How To PARENT with ADHD

Manage and Improve Your Kid's Emotional Regulation, Focus, and Self-Control

TO UNDERSTAND AND SUPPORT YOUR NEURODIVERGENT CHILD

KRISSA LAINE

© **Copyright 2024 - All rights reserved.**

The content contained within this book may not be reproduced, duplicated, or transmitted without direct written permission from the author or the publisher.

Under no circumstances will any blame or legal responsibility be held against the publisher, or author, for any damages, reparation, or monetary loss due to the information contained within this book. Either direct or indirect. You are responsible for your own choices, actions, and results.

Legal Notice:

This book is copyright protected. This book is only for personal use. You cannot amend, distribute, sell, use, quote, or paraphrase any part of the content within this book. without the consent of the author or publisher.

Disclaimer Notice:

Please note the information contained within this document is for educational and entertainment purposes only. All effort has been executed to present accurate, up-to-date, and reliable complete information No warranties of any kind are declared or implied. Readers acknowledge that the author is not engaging in the rendering of legal, financial, medical, or professional advice. The content within this book has been derived from various sources. Please consult a licensed professional before attempting any techniques outlined in this book.

By reading this document the reader agrees that under no circumstances as the author is responsible for any losses, direct or indirect. which are incurred as a result of the use of the information contained within this document, including, but not limited to, – errors. omissions, or inaccuracies.

Free Bonuses

Thank you for your purchase! As a token of our appreciation, you now have exclusive access to five invaluable bonuses designed to enhance your understanding of How to Parent Children with ADHD and support your neurodivergent child.

Here's a glimpse of what you'll receive:

1. **Journey of Understanding: A Parent's Diary on Raising Children with ADHD**
2. **Growing Together: A Progress Tracker for Parenting Children with ADHD**
3. **Deciphering ADHD: A Parent's Flowchart Guide to Identifying ADHD in Children**
4. **Tailored Connections: A Parenting Style Quiz for Parents of Children with ADHD**
5. **Delightful Bites: ADHD-Friendly Treat Recipes for Kids**

To access these bonuses, simply scan the QR code:

You can also access these valuable resources by visiting https://bit.ly/Laine-ADHD (Attention: The link is case-sensitive. Enter the link exactly as it is, with the correct uppercase and lowercase letters. Otherwise, the link will not work properly).

Support and Feedback

For feedback, questions, or if you encounter any issues, please visit the link or scan the QR code to share your thoughts and get assistance:

https://authorhelpdesk.com/support

Table of Contents

Free Bonuses 3
Support and Feedback 4
Introduction 7
Chapter 1: Understanding ADHD 9
    Defining ADHD 9
    Common Hurdles of Children with ADHD 15
    Interventions for ADHD 17
    Importance of ADHD Awareness 20
    Exercise: Determining ADHD for Parents 24

Chapter 2: Managing Behaviors 27
    Three Most Common Behaviors of ADHD 27
    Understanding Behavior Causes 34
    Patience in Behavior Management 36
    Exercise: ADHD Behavior Management 38

Chapter 3: Building Resilience in Children 41
    Defining Resilience 41
    Signs of Resilience 42
    Ways to Cultivate Resilience 43

Chapter 4: ADHD-Friendly Environment 55
    Structured Environments 55
    Sensory Needs of Children with ADHD 60
    Setting Clear Rules and Expectations 62

Chapter 5: Routines and Consistency 65
    Benefits of Consistent Routines 65
    Strategies for Daily Routines 67
    Flexibility in Routines 73

Chapter 6: Positive Reinforcement 75
Role of Positive Reinforcement 75
Employing Positive Reinforcement 77
Different Reward Types 79
Addressing Reward-Related Challenges 82
Exercise: Practicing Positive Reinforcement 84

Chapter 7: Effective Communication 87
Understanding Open Communication 87
Strategies for Understanding and Empathy 92
The Art of Clear Instructions 97

Chapter 8: Parent-Teacher Collaboration 103
Building Partnerships Between Home and School 103
Collaborating on School Accommodations 105
Exercise: Roleplaying a Parent-Teacher Conference 110

Chapter 9: Self-Care for Parents 113
Putting on Your Oxygen Mask First 113
Self-Care Strategies for Parents 117
Managing Stress 122
Exercise: The Stress Test 126

Conclusion 129

Resources 131

Techniques Recap 135

Exclusive Bonuses 139

Introduction

Many parents know the heartbreak that comes from seeing their child struggle with ADHD day after day. Sometimes, nothing seems to make a lasting difference, no matter how hard you try.

As a parent of twins diagnosed with ADHD, the feeling of being scared and alone, unsure of where to even begin helping them, is always there. Experiencing this situation firsthand revealed that traditional methods often fell short. However, thorough research, expert consultations, and a dedicated shift in parenting approaches can pave the way forward. By introducing structure, clear communication, positive reinforcement, and routine, it is achievable to create an environment where children with ADHD thrive.

This book aims to reduce the steep learning curve often accompanying understanding and parenting a child with ADHD. It presents a collection of the most effective solutions, saving you the hassle of piecing together information from various sources. Drawing from years of research and firsthand experience, you will find 48 techniques, tips, and strategies peppered throughout the entire book on how to manage your child with ADHD. It's intentionally designed this way to serve as your guide along each step of the process. This guide offers precise, tested, and practical strategies that have proven transformative for numerous families.

Equipped with the knowledge contained here, you will gain the confidence to tackle challenges head-on and lay a solid foundation for your child's success. This guide addresses fundamental topics, like identifying ADHD symptoms and crafting a child-centric supportive environment. It offers insights into optimizing physical spaces, establishing consistent routines, and setting clear behavioral expectations.

Subsequent sections delve into positive behavioral management techniques, enhancing communication, and fostering collaboration with educators. The book also provides targeted advice on developing social skills, self-regulation, and resilience in children with ADHD, emphasizing parental self-care's importance.

Relying on over a decade of experience and comprehensive research, this book delivers a treasure trove of insights, ensuring that parents are well-informed and empowered. Remember, each positive step taken resonates profoundly in a child's life. With commitment and this guide, start transforming your family's dynamic today.

Chapter 1
Understanding ADHD

Often, many assume that kids with ***attention deficit hyperactivity disorder (ADHD)*** cannot sit still in class. Yes, this could be an illustration of people with ADHD, but there is so much more to it. Like the variety of colors in a rainbow, ADHD shows itself in many different ways.

This chapter aims to clarify the realities of ADHD by debunking myths and dispelling stereotypes. A nuanced understanding of this condition will give you better support for your children through specialized compassion, guidance, and assistance.

Defining ADHD

Imagine being in a crowded room with dozens of people talking at once. Even if you try to focus on one conversation, the noise from the other discussions makes it difficult. This is a simplified example of how the mind of someone with ADHD might function. People with ADHD often have difficulty focusing on one thing because their brains are 'busy' with many thoughts and stimuli at once.

Attention deficit hyperactivity disorder, known more commonly as ADHD, is a neurodevelopmental disorder characterized by persistent difficulty focusing, managing impulsive behaviors, and controlling high activity levels. Despite past misconceptions, ADHD is now recognized as a legitimate medical condition that can affect both children and adults. Every person with ADHD is unique. Symptoms can vary in intensity and type, with some individuals more affected by attention difficulties and others by hyperactivity or impulsivity.

The prevalence of ADHD is often surprising to many people. As of 2021, the **Centers for Disease Control and Prevention (CDC)** stated that approximately 6.1 million children aged 2 to 17 in the United States had been diagnosed with ADHD. These figures are not isolated to the United States; the **World Health Organization (WHO)** estimates that around 3% to 5% of school-aged children globally have ADHD. These are sizable figures, highlighting the essential need for effective strategies to manage ADHD and support affected children and their families.

ADHD can affect children and the people in their lives. For example, children with ADHD may have trouble in school because it is hard for them to focus. They might also argue with friends because they act without thinking. Such issues related to this condition can cause stress, lower confidence, and tense relationships. But with early diagnosis, a good support network, and the right treatment, children with ADHD can lead happy and successful lives.

Debunking Myths and Stereotypes about ADHD

Understanding ADHD lies in dismantling the myths and stereotypes surrounding it. These misconceptions can lead to misjudgments, stigma, and unnecessary hardships for those with ADHD. Some of the common misconceptions about this condition include the following:

Only Hyperactive Boys have ADHD

This myth arises from the stereotypical image of a person with ADHD being a boisterous, unruly boy. In reality, ADHD manifests across genders, albeit with varied symptoms. Girls often display more subtle signs, such as inattentiveness or daydreaming, leading to underdiagnosis. Their struggles may be mistaken for character traits common to their gender rather than ADHD symptoms, emphasizing the need for a better understanding and recognition of ADHD in girls and women.

People with ADHD are Unintelligent or Lazy

ADHD affects attention and impulse control, not intellectual capability. While a person with the condition might struggle with traditional learning or organizational methods, they can exhibit exceptional creativity, problem-solving skills, and unique perspectives. Labeling them as *'lazy'* or *'unintelligent'* is not only incorrect but can also affect their self-esteem and discourage them from pursuing and unleashing their potential.

ADHD is the Result of Poor Parenting

Parenting style cannot cause ADHD. This misconception places unnecessary guilt and pressure on parents. Remember, ADHD is a neurodevelopmental disorder, not a result of environmental factors like parenting style.

Children with ADHD Eventually Outgrow It

Some children's symptoms may lessen with age, leading to the assumption that they have *'outgrown'* ADHD. However, the core symptoms often evolve and manifest differently over time. A hyperactive child might become an impulsive adult. Continuous support and understanding are still required throughout an individual's lifetime.

Recognizing ADHD Signs in Your Child

Symptoms of ADHD usually become apparent during elementary school when children are expected to sit still for long periods and focus more intently. But signs can emerge as early as age three. Below are some signs of ADHD.

Hyperactivity and Impulsivity

Always on the go, cannot sit still, seems restless or fidgety, and hyperactivity might indicate ADHD. Those with hyperactivity have trouble controlling impulsive behaviors as well. Look for:

- Constant motion and an inability to stay seated.
- Frequent running, jumping, and inappropriate climbing.
- Difficulty playing quietly or doing calm activities.
- Constantly touching things and having *"busy"* hands.
- Excessive talking and interrupting.
- Difficulty waiting their turn.
- Behavior without thinking of consequences.

Inattention

Another sign of ADHD is an ongoing struggle to pay attention. Signs of inattention include:

- Limited attention span during play, school, or chores.
- Distractibility and wandering focus during tasks.
- Avoidance of reading, homework, or activities requiring concentration.
- Not listening when spoken to directly.
- Difficulty following instructions and finishing tasks.
- Forgetting daily activities and needing reminders.
- Losing school supplies, toys, and belongings frequently.

Academic Difficulties

Since ADHD affects concentration and focus, it frequently impacts school performance. Note if your child:

- Struggles to complete classwork and homework.
- Gets poor grades that do not match their intellect.
- Requires extra help compared to classmates.

- Has behavior issues reported by the teacher.
- Forgets to turn in assignments or loses supplies.

Social Challenges

The condition can also hinder social skills and relationships. Check for:

- Difficulty making or keeping friends.
- Exclusion from groups or their peers is avoiding them.
- Struggles with sharing and cooperating.
- Interrupting conversations or being *"too loud."*
- Impulsive comments that upset others.

Other Factors

Aside from behavioral symptoms, here are other factors that you could look into to determine if your child has ADHD.

Age of Onset

ADHD symptoms typically arise before age 12, and the average age of diagnosis is seven. Other factors may be at play if behaviors did not appear in early childhood.

Frequency of Symptoms

For an ADHD diagnosis, inattention or hyperactivity should be observed frequently and be more severe than normal developmental behavior. Symptoms should be present in multiple settings like home and school.

For example, Jackson is a 7-year-old boy with issues paying attention in class. His teacher notes that he frequently stares out the window during lessons and has trouble staying seated. He gets up to sharpen his pencil or go to the bathroom multiple times per hour. At home, his parents observe similar behaviors. During family meals, he fidgets in his seat, plays with his food, and interrupts others' conversations. He has trouble focusing on homework for more than five minutes before becoming distracted.

This level of inattention and hyperactivity occurs frequently and is more severe than what is typical for Jackson's age. The fact that it is happening in both the classroom and home setting points to ADHD as a possible diagnosis.

Impact on Daily Life
Behaviors that do not significantly impair a child's daily functioning, relationships, academics, self-esteem, or home life may not indicate ADHD, even if they seem problematic. Evaluate how symptoms affect the child's overall well-being and ability to thrive.

Family History
ADHD has a genetic component and tends to run in families. Having a close relative with the condition makes a child more likely to have it.

Co-existing Conditions
Around two-thirds of those with ADHD also have other conditions like anxiety, depression, OCD, or a learning disability. Noting any other diagnoses or challenges may be helpful.

If, after reviewing the above, you suspect ADHD, schedule a comprehensive medical evaluation. It helps to get perspectives from your child's teacher, doctor, and even trusted friends. They may notice behaviors you overlook. Doctors gather behavioral histories, talk to teachers, assess cognitive function, rule out other causes, and make an official diagnosis.

While ADHD presents challenges, it is treatable, especially when caught early. With comprehensive treatment and a supportive, understanding environment, children with ADHD can thrive at home, school, and life. Trust your instincts. When you suspect a problem, seek professional guidance. Getting the right support makes a world of difference.

Common Hurdles of Children with ADHD

Kids with ADHD's mind could be compared to a butterfly, forever fluttering from one fascinating bloom to another. Imagine if that butterfly was expected to remain still on one particular flower. *Would it not find this constraint challenging? Would it not yearn to flutter off to the next enticing bloom?* This is the daily reality for those living with ADHD.

ADHD is a neurodevelopmental condition that expresses itself through boundless energy and unyielding curiosity. Its primary characteristics are the triad of inattention, hyperactivity, and impulsivity, which often lead to complex hurdles in academics, social settings, and emotional well-being. Recognizing and understanding these characteristics and challenges is your first step in learning to support those with ADHD.

Problems in School

When you have a mind that dances to the beat of its drum, conventional classrooms can seem like an unsynchronized melody. That is what academics often feel like for children with ADHD. With the ever-present call of distractions, sustaining attention during lectures becomes difficult. As a result, they might miss information or find their assignment and test performance compromised, potentially leading to frustration, low self-esteem, and feeling out of step with peers.

Hyperactivity and impulsivity can amplify these struggles. Picture the undeniable urge to talk, fidget, or leave their seats, transforming a traditional classroom into a battlefield of patience and self-control. These challenges call for an academic environment that acknowledges, accommodates, and nurtures the unique needs of children with ADHD.

Social Hurdles

Regarding human interactions, children with ADHD might often feel out of place. Their condition may lead them to interrupt conversations, dominate discussions, or even struggle to wait their turn in social games. These behaviors can create misunderstandings, often leading to unfortunate labels of rudeness, inconsiderateness, or disrespect. Such misperceptions can result in social isolation, further deepening feelings of loneliness.

Add to this mix the challenge of interpreting social cues. Imagine the difficulty of navigating the world when the maps to understand others' feelings or perspectives seem unreadable. It is a hard row to hoe, leading to added layers of complexity in forming meaningful relationships.

Emotional Difficulties

Emotionally, ADHD can feel like an intense roller coaster ride, where controlling the height and speed of emotions often seems impossible. Impulsive reactions, made worse by difficulty handling feelings such as frustration, anger, or disappointment, can create problems in personal and professional relationships.

Furthermore, the consistent struggle to keep up with the world's pace can lead to more anxiety, stress, and overwhelm, negatively impacting their daily lives and perpetuating a cycle of frustration and self-doubt.

Interventions for ADHD

Effective management of ADHD often involves a comprehensive approach that integrates various treatment methods.

Behavioral Therapy

Behavioral therapy is a type of psychotherapy that teaches concrete skills to change problematic behaviors. For ADHD, it aims to improve attention, impulse control, and organizational skills through specific interventions.

Some techniques used in behavioral therapy include:

- **Token economies.** Providing rewards *(tokens or points)* for demonstrating desired behaviors. This reinforces positive habits.
- **Modeling.** The therapist demonstrates appropriate behaviors that the child can learn to imitate.
- **Role-playing.** Practicing desired responses in simulated real-life situations. This builds skills.
- **Self-monitoring.** Having the child track their behaviors and habits to increase awareness.
- **Organizational skills training.** Learning systems like checklists and planners to stay on task.
- **Cognitive restructuring.** Identifying unhelpful thought patterns and replacing them with more adaptive thinking.

This therapy aims to improve daily functioning and reduce ADHD-related difficulties through direct coaching of relevant skills. It equips children with strategies to practice that can lead to lasting improvements in handling their condition. The goal is to teach personalized skills they can apply in the real world.

Medication

To help manage ADHD symptoms, medication is often prescribed. There are several classes of medications that work by influencing brain chemicals like *dopamine* and *norepinephrine* to improve focus, attention, and impulse control.

The main categories of ADHD medications include:

- **Stimulants.** These medications boost dopamine signaling and stimulate the central nervous system. Examples are *methylphenidate (Ritalin)* and *amphetamine/dextroamphetamine (Adderall)*.
- **Non-stimulants.** These target norepinephrine receptors and have a calming effect. Examples are *atomoxetine (Strattera), clonidine,* and *guanfacine*.
- **Antidepressants.** Certain antidepressants like *bupropion (Wellbutrin)* may be used off-label for ADHD treatment.

While medications can reduce symptoms, they also carry potential side effects like *decreased appetite, headaches, irritability,* and *sleep disturbances*. The risks and benefits need to be weighed carefully for each child. Close medical supervision is required, especially when first starting or changing dosages of ADHD medication. Be sure to consult with a professional.

Parental Education

In managing ADHD, parents have an integral role in it. They may attend educational sessions or workshops to understand ADHD better. Here, they can learn techniques to support their child at home, such as creating structured routines, using positive reinforcement, and modeling appropriate behavior.

Lifestyle Adjustments

In addition to therapy and medication, lifestyle changes can be important in managing ADHD. These modifications aim to optimize daily habits and routines to minimize symptoms.

Examples of beneficial lifestyle adjustments include:

- **Exercise.** Regular aerobic exercise helps burn excess energy and improves focus and cognitive performance. This could involve *sports, dancing, running, etc.*
- **Healthy diet.** Eating a nutritious, protein-rich diet provides the vitamins, minerals, fats, and glucose needed for optimal brain function.
- **Routine.** Maintaining consistent daily meals, homework, and bedtime schedules helps regulate energy and mood.
- **Sleep hygiene.** Prioritizing age-appropriate sleep duration. Sleep hygiene, like limiting screens before bed, can improve sleep quality.
- **Organization.** Structuring the home and workspace to minimize distractions. For example, keeping supplies in set places.

Community Support and Inspirational Figures

Remember that a diagnosis of ADHD is not a journey that one undertakes alone. Various resources exist, such as local support groups, educational materials, and online forums, where families can share experiences and offer advice.

Many successful individuals, such as *Olympic swimmer Michael Phelps, singer Justin Timberlake*, and *entrepreneur Richard Branson,* have openly discussed their ADHD diagnoses. Their stories remind us that ADHD is not a barrier to success but a unique aspect of an individual's life that can be managed and harnessed positively.

Importance of ADHD Awareness

Understanding ADHD is necessary for reframing how you respond to people living with ADHD, not just to your child. It can be easy to label the behaviors associated with ADHD as negative traits or flaws of character. Still, with understanding comes empathy, leading to a more constructive response to these behaviors. There are a lot of reasons that make understanding the condition essential. Here are some to take note of:

Fosters Empathy and Compassion

Suppose a child is constantly scolded for not paying attention or being too restless. Recognizing this action as a symptom of ADHD rather than intentional misbehavior can replace frustration with empathy. Knowledge empowers you to view these behaviors in context, providing a more compassionate response and acknowledging the person's struggles.

Provides Tailored Guidance and Support

Taking the time to learn about the nature of ADHD will give you insight into the specific challenges your child faces. Doing so allows you to provide the most effective support for them. Being able to pinpoint triggers for their difficulties helps in formulating solutions. For instance, if you recognize that your child has difficulty staying orderly, you can set up routines that make cleaning their room easier. The more knowledge you gain about ADHD, the better equipped you will be to accommodate your child's needs.

Improves Communication and Relationships

As a parent, deepening your understanding of ADHD will improve your communication and relationship with your child. When you take the time to learn about ADHD, you can have more open and understanding conversations about what your child is experiencing. This allows you to connect with them on a deeper level.

Any misconceptions you may have had can be dispelled. Such enlightenment lets you avoid stereotyping your child's behaviors and view their challenges with empathy. Knowledge of ADHD provides insight into your child's needs so you can adapt how you communicate to be most supportive.

For instance, you may shorten instructions for better focus, provide positive reinforcement, and actively listen without judgment. Making an effort to understand ADHD fosters trust and a precious connection with your child. This paves the way to a relationship built on compassion that equips you both to manage ADHD as a team.

Gives A Different Perspective

Traditionally, ADHD has been seen through a lens of deficits and challenges. However, while valid in some aspects, this perspective only shows a fraction of the whole picture. Children with ADHD possess a set of unique strengths and abilities, often overlooked and overshadowed by the difficulties they face.

Parents, educators, and society must expand this narrow view and fully appreciate these children's potential. To familiarize yourself, here are the most common strengths of children with the condition.

Creativity

When thinking of creativity, people often picture artists and writers. However, creativity, particularly in children with ADHD, is not confined to these realms. It seeps into all aspects of their lives—from unique problem-solving approaches to critical thinking and innovation in various disciplines. The unconventional thinking styles characteristic of ADHD—*leaping from one idea to another*—may seem chaotic. But when guided, this can become fertile ground for fresh insights and ground-breaking ideas.

Fueled by an intense curiosity and an undying thirst for new experiences, children with ADHD continually push the boundaries of conventional wisdom. They might stumble upon surprising connections and patterns in their relentless quest for fresh information. This kind of exploration fosters a rich, creative thinking environment.

While creativity is a notable strength in children with ADHD, it is not a golden ticket to success. They often grapple with executive functions like planning, organization, and time management, making translating their brilliant ideas into tangible accomplishments challenging. For these creative powerhouses to develop, create strategies to manage these challenges while effectively capitalizing on their creative potential.

Persistent

In the face of challenges, children with ADHD have an awe-inspiring persistence. Once their sights are set on a goal, they can exhibit an unwavering commitment, demonstrating resilience and an uncanny ability to bounce back from setbacks.

Visualize a child with ADHD with a passion for sports. Their fiery drive and stubborn dedication could lead them to spend hours honing their skills, constantly pushing their boundaries, and refusing to accept defeat. This tenacious spirit can result in personal victories and growth that extend beyond the playing field, teaching valuable life skills such as goal setting, planning, and unyielding determination.

Nurturing their inherent persistence can help develop essential life skills and resilience. As a parent, you must equip them with the tools and resources to navigate challenges and setbacks effectively. Doing so empowers your child to thrive academically, professionally, and personally.

Extremely Energetic

Children with ADHD have this liveliness that fuels their actions and thoughts. This boundless energy, one of their most prominent characteristics, propels them to multitask and be perpetually on the move. It is like an inexhaustible engine, generating a drive and determination that helps them surmount challenges and persist even in adversity.

Pair this energy with a passion for exploration, and you have an enthusiastic explorer ready to embrace new ideas and experiences. This excitement is not just internal; it spreads outwards, affecting those around them and prompting them to view the world through a fresh lens and seize novel opportunities. In a collaborative environment, this unwavering enthusiasm can sustain and maintain motivation throughout a project, making children with ADHD excellent team members.

Such intensity and drive can position them as natural leaders, inspiring others to rally behind their shared vision and passion. However, their energy levels can sometimes be overwhelming for others, thus necessitating the development of skills to balance and manage this intensity.

This high energy can also pose challenges. While it allows for versatility, it often manifests as restlessness and impulsivity. Consequently, these children might struggle with focusing on a single task, making prioritization and time management difficult. But with the right guidance, this energy can be channeled constructively, turning a potential challenge into a potent strength.

Exercise: Determining ADHD for Parents

There are some noticeable signs of attention deficit hyperactivity disorder *(ADHD)*. This exercise will guide you through some of these behaviors often associated with the condition. However, remember this is merely an observational exercise, not a formal diagnostic tool. Consult a healthcare professional for a thorough evaluation.

Instructions

Over the next two weeks, take some time each day to observe your child in various environments and during different activities. Keep a journal, and note down any instances of the following behaviors:

- **Inattention.** Does your child have difficulty staying on task, often leaving projects unfinished? Do they forget instructions or misplace their belongings frequently? Do they often seem not to listen when spoken to directly?
- **Hyperactivity.** Does your child seem constantly on the go, as if driven by a motor? Do they fidget, tap, or squirm when seated for a while? Do they talk excessively?
- **Impulsivity.** Does your child often interrupt conversations or activities? Do they have trouble waiting their turn? Do they often act without thinking about the consequences of their actions?

Scoring

Count the number of times you observe each behavior. Normally, children display these behaviors occasionally. But in the case of ADHD, these behaviors are more frequent and severe than in other children of the same age.

- **Few instances (less than six instances in a week).** Typical child behavior, but continue observing.
- **Moderate instances (6 to 14 instances in a week).** Might need to investigate further. It may still be within normal limits, but it would not hurt to consult a professional.
- **Many instances (15 or more instances in a week).** Consult a healthcare professional for a thorough evaluation.

Note

Remember that this exercise is a basic observational tool and does not replace a professional diagnosis. ADHD is a complex disorder, and its diagnosis involves a comprehensive evaluation by trained medical professionals who consider several factors, including the child's medical history, school performance, behavior in different settings, and more. If your child consistently displays behaviors related to inattention, hyperactivity, or impulsivity, consult a healthcare provider. Early diagnosis and intervention can make a significant difference in managing ADHD and supporting your child's development.

Chapter 2
Managing Behaviors

Children with ADHD are in constant motion, do impulsive actions, and have a lack of focus. Experiencing these daily behaviors could drain your mental and emotional bandwidth as parents.

But seeing these behaviors as symptoms of a disorder outside your child's control would help. With consistent effort built on a foundation of love and wisdom, you will be able to manage difficult behaviors in constructive ways.

To get started, this chapter will begin with an overview of the three most common ADHD behaviors you may encounter. The latter part encompasses specific techniques to deal with those behaviors effectively.

Three Most Common Behaviors of ADHD

As mentioned earlier, every child with ADHD is unique. How their characteristics manifest and intensity can vary significantly from child to child. Recognizing these nuances can help parents, teachers, and caregivers approach each child, offering the right support and strategies to help them.

The three main behaviors common in children with ADHD are the following:

Inattention

Inattention, in the context of ADHD, does not merely mean an inability to focus on a task. It is a pervasive and disruptive problem, often manifesting as forgetfulness, difficulty sustaining attention, or inability to complete tasks.

Consider Jenny, a bright twelve-year-old student. Despite her intelligence, she often struggles to keep up in school. She frequently forgets her assignments, has difficulty organizing her work, and struggles to follow instructions. Often, she will start a project only to drift off partway, leaving it unfinished. This isn't due to a lack of trying or laziness; rather, it is a symptom of the inattention component of ADHD.

Manifestations of Inattention

Inattention in children with ADHD often extends beyond the typical forgetfulness or distractibility associated with childhood. This component can manifest in:

- **Challenges in focusing.** Children with ADHD often struggle to concentrate on tasks that are routine, mundane, or demand sustained mental effort. They might frequently switch from one activity to another, failing to finish what they start.
- **Forgetfulness.** Children with ADHD may often forget to do their homework or chores. They might also frequently misplace their belongings, such as toys, books, or school materials.
- **Difficulty with organization.** Keeping track of assignments or organizing their belongings can be tough for children with ADHD. Their rooms, desks, or school bags might often be messy and chaotic.

- **Struggle with following instructions.** Despite understanding the directions, children with ADHD may find it hard to follow through without getting sidetracked, leading to incomplete tasks.

Coping with Inattention

The inability to focus and stay on task is a hallmark of ADHD and perhaps the most disruptive to learning. Managing inattention takes effort but it is possible. Experiment to find out what environment and motivational strategies produce the best focus from your child. Here are several strategies can help minimize problems with inattention:

- **Reduce distractions.** Have your child work in a quiet space away from noise, windows, TV, people, and clutter. Some children focus better with gentle background noise, like calm music. Do this by removing electronics. Phones, TVs, and tablets can cause divided attention. Restrict device use during study and work times.
- **Give one task at a time.** Only give one direction at once. Multi-step instructions can be overwhelming. Break big projects down into smaller tasks.
- **Use timers and alarms.** Set a timer for chunks of work time, like 30 minutes. Bells, kitchen timers, or alarms on phones or watches can signal time to take a break or switch tasks.
- **Write it down.** Have your child write down assignment instructions, due dates, and steps involved in big projects. Referring to the notes helps combat forgetfulness.
- **Do the tough stuff first.** Tackle harder work like math and reading when your child's focus is best— often early in the day. Save easier or more enjoyable work for later.
- **Incorporate movement.**

- **Check often for understanding.** Ask questions frequently to keep them engaged. Have them repeat the instructions. Reinforce listening skills.
- **Offer praise.** When you catch your child demonstrating prolonged focus, let them know. Praise good behavior and effort. This can motivate them.
- **Add accountability.** Check work frequently for neatness, accuracy, and completeness. Review their assignment notebook. Follow up with teachers.

Hyperactivity

Hyperactivity goes beyond just having a lot of energy. Hyperactive people often feel a near-constant need to move or do something.

Manifestations of Hyperactivity

Hyperactivity in children with ADHD translates into an almost constant state of motion and excessive energy. This component includes:

- **Physical restlessness.** Children with ADHD might frequently fidget, squirm in their seats, or run and climb when it is inappropriate. They may find it challenging to engage in leisure activities quietly, such as reading a book.
- **Excessive talking.** These children often talk excessively and have difficulty engaging in activities quietly. Unaware that they often dominate conversations.
- **Impatience.** Experience difficulties waiting for their turn in games or group activities due to the constant need for movement.
- **Impulsive physical actions.** Children with ADHD tend to engage in more accidental behavior, like bumping into things or knocking items over. *They act first and think later.*

- **"Busy" behavior.** Constantly occupied with something, even if it is productive or not. With this behavior, children with ADHD might rush through tasks or activities.
- **Difficulty playing quietly.** There is always a thrive on constant stimulation for children with ADHD. Sitting down for calm activities like reading, coloring, or puzzles may be hard for your hyperactive child.

Managing Hyperactive Behaviors

Hyperactivity is a core characteristic of ADHD. Excess energy and motion can be very disruptive at home and school. While it usually improves over time, managing hyperactive behaviors in your child requires patience and creativity. The key is trying different techniques consistently to see what helps channel their urge to move in a productive way. Here are some tips to help:

- **Schedule plenty of activity breaks.** Let your child release pent-up energy during lengthy tasks by taking a quick break every 20 to 30 minutes. A few jumping jacks, shooting hoops, or sprinting around the house can get their wiggles out. Ensure to set a timer and limit break time.
- **Alternate high-energy and calming activities.** Follow active playtime with slower activities like coloring, reading books, or doing puzzles. Help them transition between energetic and relaxed states.
- **Limit distractions during tasks.** Seat your child away from windows, doorways, and noise when they are working on schoolwork. Reduce visual clutter on walls and desks. Soft music or a fan sound may actually help drown out distracting noises.
- **Incorporate fidget items.** Let your child keep small fidget toys like stress balls, bendable snakes, or modeling clay at their desk to occupy restless hands. Simple doodling can also help channel excess energy.

- **Allow opportunities for movement.** Your child may focus better while standing at times, so offer this option. Treadmills or bicycle desks allow motion while working. Frame chores as movement opportunities.
- **Get active together.** Schedule regular family play time outdoors at the park, biking or kicking a ball around. Join your child in releasing energy through movement they enjoy.
- **Enforce bedtimes.** Adequate sleep is key for better behavior control. Set and enforce a regular bedtime to keep your child well-rested.

Impulsivity

Impulsivity in ADHD can be described as acting without thinking about the consequences.

Manifestation of Impulsivity

Children with ADHD often have difficulty waiting, interrupt conversations, or make hasty decisions, resulting in behaviors that may seem careless or risky. This behavior can include:

- **Interrupting.** Children with ADHD often find waiting their turn during conversations or games hard, leading to frequent interruptions or intrusions.
- **Impulsive behavior.** These children might make quick decisions without considering the potential fallout, like running across the street without looking or touching things they have been instructed not to touch.
- **Difficulty with emotional control.** Kids with ADHD struggle to manage their emotional responses, often leading to outbursts or reactions that seem disproportionate to the situation.

Curbing Impulsive Behaviors

The inability to control impulses is a major obstacle for kids with ADHD. They often act first and think later. You can help temper impulsivity with patience, preparation, and clear expectations:

- **Use waiting strategies.** Teach techniques like counting to 10, taking deep breaths, squeezing a stress ball, or visualization. Practice waiting for short intervals to build patience.
- **Reward patience.** Praise successful waits, taking turns, and good decisions. Small rewards like stickers motivate them to repeat good behavior.
- **Implement structured routines.** Follow set schedules for meals, homework, bedtime, and chores. Consistent routines encourage thinking before acting.
- **Avoid quick triggers.** Limit time in tempting situations like toy stores. Have snacks on hand to curb impulsive eating.
- **Use positive reinforcement.** When you notice good impulse control, offer immediate praise and incentives.
- **Provide fidget outlets.** Keep toys like stress balls and Play-Doh nearby to occupy impulsive hands. Simple doodling can help too.
- **Use logical consequences.** Impulsive actions should result in natural consequences, not just punishment. Explain the why behind outcomes.
- **Change the environment.** Remove temptations and distractions from your child's surroundings when possible. This removes impulsive triggers.
- **Act as a model.** Demonstrate thoughtful decision-making in yourself and others. *Be the example.*
- **Keep your cool.** A calm response is more effective than anger. React patiently and use it as a teaching moment.
- **Consider therapy.** For severe impulsivity, therapy like cognitive behavioral therapy can teach coping skills.

Understanding Behavior Causes

Getting frustrated when your child acts out with tantrums, defiance, or lack of compliance is normal. But when you take time to understand the root motivations driving behaviors, you gain eye-opening insight.

While consequences still have their place in enforcing discipline, your first reaction should be focused on understanding rather than just controlling behaviors. When kids feel deeply understood, they become more receptive to guidance.

Common motivational factors include:

Unmet Sensory Needs

For many neurodivergent children, behaviors reflect efforts to self-regulate in response to sensory overstimulation or deprivation. Fidgeting, vocal outbursts, or withdrawal may be their best attempt to generate needed input or limit intake. Tantrums often arise when kids feel sensory overload but cannot articulate or adapt. Once you understand their unique sensory needs, you can modify environments proactively to prevent issues. Accommodating sensitivities to noise, textures, personal space, and other stimuli reduces behavioral struggles.

Executive Functioning Challenges

Behaviors like disorganization, forgetting homework, poor time management, and difficulty completing multi-step tasks often stem from impairments in executive functioning skills. These include working memory, organization, planning, prioritization, and self-control.

Remember, children are not choosing to ignore expectations—they genuinely lack the developmental capacity to manage complex responsibilities without extensive scaffolding and support. Have a deep understanding of their skills profile so that you can manage expectations and set your kid up for success.

Pursuit of Connection

Attention-provoking behaviors can signal an underlying craving for parental connection. Children with ADHD often annoy siblings, talk back, or purposely break the rules to seek engagement and one-on-one. These children need increased opportunities to receive positive attention, bonding, and reinforcement so they do not feel forced to misbehave or have someone interact with them.

Fatigue and Hunger

When basic self-care needs like nutrition, hydration, and sleep are unmet, children have far less capacity to maintain behavioral and emotional control. Ensuring proper nutrition, minimizing hunger or thirst, and prioritizing ample nighttime sleep prevents many sensory and emotional outbursts.

Feeling Overwhelmed

Task demands that exceed a child's intrinsic capabilities often lead to avoidance behaviors, distraction tactics, or acting out. Neurodivergent kids process instructions and responsibilities differently. By simplifying language, providing models, and thoughtfully matching tasks to skill level, kids avoid feeling inundated and the behaviors that may follow.

Anxiety Triggers

Unexpected transitions, unfamiliar social situations, schedule disruptions, and forced social interactions can cause anxious behaviors in many neurodivergent children. Tantrums, resistance, withdrawal, and defiance often signify an underlying anxiety response. Accommodating needs around newness, unpredictability, and pacing of social interactions can prevent many behavioral struggles.

Patience in Behavior Management

As a parent of a child with ADHD, patience helps model self-control and allows your child to improve hard-to-manage behaviors gradually. Progress often comes slowly, with frequent setbacks that may test you. But resisting the urge to overreact keeps you moving in the right direction.

Benefits of Patience

Progress requires praising small wins, not just criticizing mistakes. Patience helps you maintain an encouraging, supportive mindset over the ups and downs of the process. Other benefits include:

- Models self-control and maturity. Kids learn from your example. Staying calm shows important regulation.
- Allows time for your child to develop and practice new skills gradually.
- Prevents escalation of problematic behaviors that result from anger or criticism.
- Allowing you to better evaluate the reasons and motivations behind your child's behavior before reacting.
- Encourages your child to build persistence and resilience when faced with challenges. They will mimic your steady persistence.

- Strengthens your relationship and keeps communication open through difficult times.

Tips for Being Patient

Patience is often easier said than done in the face of frustration. But it can be strengthened through purposeful practice. Here are tips:

- **Take deep breaths when you feel your anger rising.** Pause before responding. Step out of the room if necessary.
- **Focus on the progress your child has made, even if small.** Reflecting on their improvement motivates continued patience.
- **Expect that setbacks will happen as part of the process.** Do not overreact to periodic backsliding or mistakes.
- **Share your struggles with your partner, friends, or other ADHD parents.** They can relate and help you vent safely.
- **Take breaks from parenting duties when possible.** Let your co-parent take over for a while. Prioritize self-care.
- **Notice and celebrate when your child succeeds at something they have struggled with.** Praise builds momentum.
- **Use mantras.** Say something like "Progress over perfection" and "Respond, do not react" to cue yourself to remain calm.
- **Model apologizing after losing your cool.** Doing so will teach your child how to make amends.
- **Focus on solutions, not just problems.** If one strategy is not working, explore alternatives.
- **Show compassion.** Remember, your child is not giving you a hard time but having a hard time. Empathy goes a long way.

- **Pick your battles and compromise when practical.** Let minor issues slide at times.

Raising a child with ADHD tests even the most patient parent. But by making patience a daily practice—*just like a workout routine*—you can build your capacity to remain calm and consistent through this journey.

Exercise: ADHD Behavior Management

Below are 10 hypothetical scenarios involving common ADHD-related behaviors. Read each scenario and take a moment to consider how you would react in a calm, constructive manner. Jot down a few notes on your response.

1. During homework time, your 7-year-old child is restless, frequently standing to play with toys or gazing out the window. Gentle reminders to resume their seat are met with either neglect or resistance.
2. While conversing with a friend, your child persistently interrupts despite being repeatedly asked to wait. They impulsively interject, disregarding your requests for conversational etiquette.
3. Approaching bedtime, you discover your child energetically jumping on their bed for the third time this week, directly violating established household rules meant for winding down.
4. As you prepare to leave for school, your child adamantly refuses to wear their jacket despite the chilly weather. Any attempt to dress them results in a game of chase.
5. Having issued two prior reminders, you find your child's bicycle discarded on the lawn while they are engrossed in video games indoors.

6. Amidst dinner preparations, your child repeatedly interrupts you to share trivial anecdotes. Despite being asked to wait, the interruptions persist.
7. At school pickup, the teacher informs you that your child's excessive silliness disrupted the day's educational activities. This marks the third occurrence of such behavior this week.
8. When invited to join a family board game, your child opts for tablet play and resists the 30-minute pre-bedtime screen limit, leading to an ongoing debate.
9. After requesting that your child prepare for bed by donning pajamas and brushing their teeth, you find them 20 minutes later still engrossed in play, wearing their daytime attire.
10. During dinner, your child incessantly drums on the table with their hands. Despite two previous requests to cease, the rhythmic disturbance continues.

Reflecting on how to react calmly and consistently prepares you to handle real-life situations better. Over time, you will get better at constructively managing ADHD behaviors. Remember to breathe, stay solution-focused, and praise progress.

Chapter 3
Building Resilience in Children

Every parent wants their children to grow into confident, capable adults who can bounce back from life's inevitable setbacks. The good news is that resilience can be fostered from an early age. Research shows resilient kids share optimism, adaptability, and strong social connections. The even better news is that these traits can be developed in children.

Though ADHD brings unique hurdles, it also brings unique gifts. Your child may be wired differently, but great perseverance and inner strength lie within them. By nurturing resilience, you can empower them to cope with challenges and thrive because of them.

In this chapter, you will learn practical strategies to promote resilience in your neurodivergent kid. This chapter will also show how to reframe challenges as opportunities for growth.

Defining Resilience

A parent's instinct is to protect their children from facing any struggles or adversity. But the reality is *growing up brings inevitable challenges*. For children with ADHD who already face extra hurdles, the path can be more challenging. However, you can equip your kid to develop resilience to overcome obstacles and return from such challenges.

What is Resilience?

Resilience is the quality that allows people to recover from setbacks, learn from failure, and become better for the experience. But it is more than just getting through tough times. Resilient individuals can adapt, grow, and even thrive in the face of challenges.

Children with ADHD likely struggle to manage their symptoms, schoolwork, focus, emotions, and social situations. Yet, this resilience is like a muscle that grows stronger with training and practice. You can coach your children to build mental strength and flexibility when faced with challenges. This involves focusing on their abilities, reframing setbacks as growth opportunities, and providing tools to tackle difficulties.

Signs of Resilience

Resilience manifests in kids through certain attitudes and behaviors. Being attuned to these qualities empowers you to cultivate them further. Here are some key signs of resilience to watch for:

- **Optimism.** Kids who can maintain a generally hopeful perspective and positive attitude demonstrate resilience even when facing difficulties. The ability to see setbacks as temporary rather than personal failures denotes mental flexibility and grit. *Encourage optimism by reframing challenges, focusing on progress, and reminding kids they have overcome before.*
- **Adaptability.** Resilient kids can demonstrate cognitive, emotional, and behavioral flexibility when navigating changing circumstances. Where rigid thinking causes anxiety, adaptable kids can shift their mindsets and modulate emotions and actions appropriately. *Teach adaptability by highlighting life's ever-changing nature and encouraging versatile responses.*

- **Problem-Solving Skills.** Being able to analyze issues and strategize solutions independently shows crucial resilience. Kids who avoid jumping to conclusions and can brainstorm plans point to strong logic and self-direction. *Develop these skills by modeling careful deliberation and walking kids through a step-by-step problem-solving process.*
- **Self-Efficacy.** A resilient sense of self-efficacy refers to believing in one's fundamental abilities to handle difficulties. Kids who know they possess innate strengths and can become capable exhibit greater resilience. *Instill self-belief by emphasizing past successes, framing capabilities as learnable skills, and conveying unconditional confidence.*
- **Help-Seeking.** Knowing when to seek external support, whether from trusted adults, peers, or professionals, demonstrates resilient wisdom. Kids who balance independence with appropriate help-seeking when overwhelmed exhibit crucial discernment. *Encourage wise help-seeking by normalizing needing support, applauding it, and building a support group.*

Ways to Cultivate Resilience

As a parent, how can you help empower resilience in our children with ADHD? There are many practical strategies you can use day-to-day, such as:

Foster a Positive Mindset

Children's perspective on themselves and the world informs how they approach life's ups and downs. The following strategies will empower your kids to have a positive mental outlook, leading to resiliency.

Instill Hope

As parents, hope is one of the greatest gifts you can give your children. To instill hope, introduce your child to stories of individuals, especially those with ADHD, who have overcome challenges and found success.

Real-life examples or characters from books and movies can inspire hope and determination. Statements like, *"Remember how that character faced a similar challenge and overcame it?"* can make a difference.

Initiate also a *'Hope Journal'* to write down hopes, dreams, and even worries. Revisit the journal to see how many hopes and dreams have been realized or are on their way to being achieved. This practice gives your child something to look forward to and provides tangible evidence that things do get better, further instilling hope.

Focus on Strengths

Make it a priority to regularly observe, identify, and verbalize your child's positive qualities and abilities. When their strengths are highlighted, their confidence grows. Assign tasks that allow them to apply their talents. Say things like, *"I see how you used your creativity to come up with a solution."* Linking successes back to strengths develops self-assurance.

Reframe Setbacks as Learning Opportunities

When setbacks happen, reframe these as opportunities for growth and avoid harsh criticism. Instead, reframe it as a chance to gain insight. Say things like, *"Now you know for next time"* or *"Mistakes help us improve."* Model turning failures into future success yourself. Children learn to bounce back faster when they believe abilities can be developed.

Aside from that, collaborate with your child to brainstorm potential solutions. Walk them through weighing the pros and cons and encourage them to choose. Such a hands-on approach allows them to experience the process of navigating challenges, fostering a belief that obstacles are beatable.

Encourage Positive Self-talk

Children's inner dialogue impacts their resilience. Teach your child to counter negative thoughts with empowering statements like *"I can get through this"* or *"I will try a different strategy."* Make this a daily habit, having them repeat affirmations. Their self-perception changes when they override pessimism with possibility thinking.

Discuss also the idea that abilities and intelligence can grow with effort. Help them understand that every challenge they face is an opportunity to stretch and grow. Use phrases like, *"Every effort you put in brings you one step closer to getting better at it."*

Develop Their Problem-Solving Skills

Parents have this instinct to fix the problems for their children. However, this can rob kids of building critical life skills like independent problem-solving. Problem-solving helps build resilience in children to work through anything challenging that comes their way.

Incorporate the step-by-step coaching approach below to help your kid gain the confidence to analyze, attempt solutions, and reevaluate when things do not go smoothly.

1. **Break the problem down.** Identify one small, manageable piece of the problem to focus on together. Doing so makes big or abstract challenges feel less overwhelming.

2. **Walk through possible solutions.** Verbally discuss options and possibilities without giving them the answer directly.
   - **Tip:** Ask open-ended questions like *"What have you tried so far?"* and *"What do you think would happen if you did X?"* This scaffolds their thinking while letting them retain ownership of the problem.
3. **Give them plenty of room to try and fail.** With your support and guidance in the background, allow them to attempt solutions themselves. Reinforce that making mistakes is part of the learning process. Praise their effort, not just the result.
4. **Avoid taking over.** Avoid constantly monitoring their progress. Well-intentioned checking in can sometimes send the subtle message that you do not believe they can work through challenges independently. If they ask for your help, encourage them to explain exactly where they are stuck before you provide suggestions. This helps strengthen their analytical skills.
5. **Praise the process.** Focus on praising their hard work and perseverance, not just the outcome. Affirmations such as, *"I'm proud of you no matter what,"* provide a safety net, making them feel secure even in the face of setbacks.

Build Support Systems

Humans are innately social beings and thrive in communities. Close ties with family, friends, and community give your kid a vital support system. By guiding them to nurture healthy relationships, you surround them with encouragement to lean on.

Building Strong Family Ties

For children with ADHD who may feel misunderstood by others, positive family relationships are essential. As their first community, the family set the tone. With close family ties, your child gains a safe haven. Home becomes their place to recharge when the world feels harsh.

Follow these tips to help your child establish close family ties.

- **Express warmth and unconditional love through words, hugs, and quality time.** Ensure your child knows they are accepted just as they are.
- **Keep everyone involved.** Family meals, board game nights, or reading before bed are powerful bonding opportunities. Small moments like walking together after dinner or sharing weekend chores deepen connections.
- **Share family stories that convey shared values like perseverance.** Talk about relatives who have overcome challenges.
- **Model healthy communication** like taking turns, listening without judgment, and managing anger. Set the example of working through conflict.
- **Find opportunities for one-on-one time with your child,** whether chatting over breakfast or playing a board game together.

Building Friendships with Peers

Positive friendships can provide a protective buffer against life's challenges. With some guidance, your child can develop the social skills to nurture meaningful friendships. These will support them through thick and thin.

As parents, you can help facilitate these relationships by doing the following:

- **Set up play dates** with patient peers your child connects with. Coordinate activities around their interests, like baking cookies or playing basketball. This provides a comfortable setting to practice social skills.
- **Role-play scenarios** to rehearse friendship building, like introducing themselves, sharing toys, or extending invitations. Provide feedback and praise their effort.
- **Find peers with similar passions** like art, chess, or video games. Bonding over common interests lays the foundation for friendship.
- **Enroll your child in groups or clubs centered around their hobbies.** Being with like-minded peers helps them feel a sense of belonging.
- **Use TV shows or books to spark conversations** about inclusiveness, kindness, and peer pressure. Help them reflect on what makes a good friend.

Building Communal Ties

A well-known phrase says, *"It takes a village to raise a child."* This saying underscores the idea that a child's upbringing and development are a collective effort. For children with ADHD who face added challenges, a strong support network is priceless.

To ensure that your kid gets the extended support they need, do the following:

- **Get involved in community groups** like Scouts, sports teams, or theater where your child can discover their passions. Positive role models and mentors matter.

- **Look into ADHD support groups** for parents and kids. Connecting with others on the same journey provides a vital sense of community.
- **Explore youth mentoring programs** that match teens with ADHD with caring adult volunteers who provide guidance.
- **Find an experienced therapist or coach** who can teach kids healthy coping strategies. Ongoing mental health support is calming.
- At school, **collaborate with teachers** to put accommodations in place. Consistent allies at home and school provide stability.
- **Ask for help.** Seek out family, friends, and professionals who can lend an extra hand or a listening ear when needed.

Exemplify Resilience Yourself

Children see their parents as their primary resilience role models. Through your instruction and demonstration, kids learn how to persevere, problem-solve, and maintain hope. By exemplifying resilience in handling adversity ourselves, you provide the living blueprint for our child to internalize.

Let your child observe firsthand how you bounce back from life's challenges and cultivate a growth mindset. Verbalize your inner thought processes and coping strategies out loud. For example, when frustrations arise, say things like:

- *"I am feeling discouraged, but I am going to take deep breaths and look for a different solution."*
- *"The situation is upsetting, but I have overcome setbacks like this and will again."*
- *"I will learn from this mistake and try a new approach next time."*

Being authentic and experiencing emotions like sadness, anger, and anxiety in difficult times while modeling how you work through them with resilience teaches your child that hardship is conquerable. This resilience will permeate their spirit and give them the courage to say, *"If you can do it, I can too."*

To further exemplify this, share age-appropriate stories about times you persevered through serious challenges in your life. Discuss what helped you cope and maintain hope even when things looked bleak. Your lived wisdom provides guiding light.

Point out also small acts of everyday resilience you practice, like apologizing for mistakes, seeking help when needed, and looking at situations optimistically. Children learn more from real-life actions than from lectures about resilience.

Lastly, admit moments when you fall short of resilience—*snapping in anger, wallowing in worry, avoiding challenges.* Then, verbalize your plan to get back on track—this models imperfection and correction.

Encourage Self-Confidence

Children with ADHD often struggle with low self-esteem due to difficulties in school, relationships, and managing symptoms. As their cheerleader, help them build their confidence.

Strategies for Promoting Confidence

For children with ADHD, school may be a daily battleground littered with comparisons to peers, leading to self-doubt to sink in.

But confidence can be nurtured. With intentionality and care, you can grow our children's belief in themselves by leaps and bounds. To do so, do the following:

Identify Strengths

Children's strengths form the foundation for their self-confidence. Tuning into their natural abilities and reinforcing what they do well plant the seeds of belief in their potential.

In identifying your child's strengths, list their positive qualities, talents, interests, and skills. Include creativity, sense of humor, persistence, athletic ability, intelligence, musicality, kindness, and courage. Consult teachers, family members, and friends for their observations of your child's strengths.

Keep this list somewhere noticeable, like on the fridge or bulletin board, so you can continuously add to it and remind your child of all the wonderful things they possess. Revisit it yourself when you are feeling discouraged to recall everything your child brings to the table. Update it as your child gets older and develops new strengths. Seeing all their strengths listed out fosters pride and belief in themselves.

Align Tasks with Their Strengths

After noting your child's strengths and abilities, develop activities and tasks that allow them to apply their talents. For a creative child, sign them up for an arts camp or community theater group. When your child is musically gifted, explore guitar or piano lessons. Meanwhile, if your child is more athletic, look into a local basketball or soccer league.

Provide opportunities for them to cultivate what comes naturally to breed success and confidence. At home, assign chores that align with strengths too. Leverage their organization skills by having them keep the pantry tidy or their artistic eye by letting them decorate the family bulletin board. When strengths are utilized, their self-esteem blossoms. They realize they have much to contribute and take pride in doing their part.

Always remember to seek feedback from your child on what they feel are their strengths. Collaborate on brainstorming how to create experiences centered around them.

Give Strengths-Based Praise
Using praise to draw attention to children's unique strengths is a powerful way to foster self-confidence. When you verbalize the positive ways they are leveraging their talents and abilities, it reinforces their competence and belief in themselves.

Get in the habit of linking your child's efforts and accomplishments to their strengths. For example, *"I saw how you stuck with that math worksheet until it was complete—you showed real focus today!"* or *"The way you comforted your brother demonstrated so much empathy and kindness."*

Be specific so they know exactly which strengths enabled their success. Some may come more naturally, while others need practice. Praise any use of strengths, from small to big. For instance, *"I know it is hard for you to sit still, but I noticed how you tried your best to focus during story time— great job sticking with it!"*

Over time, **continually highlighting their strengths** in action helps these skills become second nature. Their self-talk shifts from doubt to affirmations like *"I can do this!"* They internalize the message that they have what it takes to succeed through the unique combination of talents that makes them who they are.

Set Achievable Goals

Setting challenging yet attainable goals helps build resilience in children. When goals feel just beyond reach, they require focused effort and perseverance. Working toward these meaningful targets teaches kids to cope and bounce back from inevitable setbacks.

Pay attention to each child's evolving needs and abilities in setting goals. With the right balance of structure, encouragement, and flexibility, goal-setting teaches invaluable skills. Kids learn to take manageable risks, appreciate incremental gains, and develop resilience when faced with challenges. Most importantly, achievable goals give children a sense of empowerment over their development and a belief in their limitless potential.

Involve your child in picking their goals based on their unique interests and abilities. Ask them what they like to learn or accomplish, from specific skills like riding a bike to broader achievements like performing well academically. Goals children help shape will have more meaning and motivation behind them.

Besides that, ***match goals to your child's current developmental level*** so they represent a challenge but feel within realistic reach. Goals that seem unattainable from the outset set kids up for frustration. As they accomplish smaller goals, you can gradually raise the bar. Periodically re-evaluate and adjust goals as needed to provide this continuous, optimal level of stretch.

Chapter 4
ADHD-Friendly Environment

As a plant needs the right soil, sunlight, and water to thrive, your child needs an environment that suits them. And for kids with ADHD, this environment might look a bit different from what seemed typical for other children.

The first topic in this chapter is the structured environments for people with ADHD. Aside from that, this chapter will touch on the sensory needs that your child may need. It will explore what this means and how to incorporate it into your child's environment.

But remember, this is not about creating a *'perfect'* environment. Instead, you are building a supportive, accommodating, and understanding environment that meets your child's unique needs.

Structured Environments

Creating an ADHD-friendly environment is about building a personal space for your child. Such an environment does not need to be aesthetically pleasing like the one in the magazines. Instead, aim for a place that evokes calm and tranquility and feels welcoming to your child.

With thoughtful planning, a well-designed room can contribute significantly to helping your child focus, stay organized, and feel more in control of their surroundings. Some techniques to help you build this safe space are listed below.

Decluttering

Clutter, in many ways, can mirror mental chaos. Especially for a child with ADHD, a messy space teems with distractions that can pull their attention in all directions. Streamlining and organizing their space reduces these distractions and helps them concentrate better.

When decluttering, approach it as a fun activity you and your child can engage in together. This joint venture not only gives you quality time together but also serves as an excellent opportunity to teach organizational skills. Plus, having a hand in shaping their space gives your child a sense of control, which can be incredibly empowering for them.

Tips for decluttering:

- **Establish Zones.** Create specific areas for different activities. For instance, a clear desk for homework, a cozy corner for reading, and a spacious floor area for play. Having separate zones can help your child know what is expected in each area and stay focused on the task.
- **Use Storage Systems.** Invest in simple storage systems such as bins, shelves, and containers. Label them clearly to help your child know where things belong, making it easier for them to keep their spaces tidy.
- **Regular Clean-Up.** Set a regular clean-up time. It could be 10 minutes at the end of each day or a longer session once a week.

Comfort

For an environment to be inviting, the feeling of comfort for your child to engage in tasks without physical discomfort distracting them is necessary. Adding ergonomics like a supportive chair or a desk at the right height can make a difference. Incorporate also soft cushions for your child to lean into while reading or an area rug inviting them to sit and focus on a task.

Tips for creating a comfortable space:

- **Test Out Furniture.** When choosing furniture, if possible, let your child try it out first. The right chair or table for them is the one they find most comfortable.
- **Flexible Seating Options.** Consider offering multiple seating options. Some kids with ADHD find that movement helps them concentrate, so items like yoga balls or wobble chairs can be great choices.
- **Personalize.** Make the space theirs. Let them choose some decor or arrange their desk how they like. This sense of ownership can make them feel more comfortable and invested in their space.

Lighting

A brightly lit area for homework ensures your child does not have to strain their eyes, while a softer glow might be perfect for a cozy reading nook. Natural light is also incredibly beneficial, so arrange workspaces near windows.

Lighting also regulates internal body clocks or circadian rhythms, which can often be irregular in children with ADHD. The right balance of natural and artificial light can help control these rhythms, supporting better sleep and wakefulness patterns.

Other Illuminating techniques to try:

- **Maximize Natural Light.** Arrange your child's workspace near windows to make the most of natural light, but be mindful of potential distractions from the window.
- **Adjustable Lighting.** Consider installing adjustable lighting to alter the brightness depending on the time of day or the task.
- **Experiment with Colors.** Some colors can affect mood and concentration. Generally, cool colors like blue or green are calming, while warm colors like yellow can stimulate creativity.

Room or Area

Children with ADHD often have an innate need for movement. This energy can be a fantastic resource if channeled correctly. Consider creating designated areas where your child can move freely without causing disruption. Place a small yoga mat for stretches or a mini trampoline for short, energizing bounce breaks.

Allowing for movement is not just about managing energy levels; it is about acknowledging your child's need for physical activity and incorporating it into their environment. Regular movement can boost mood, improve focus, and enhance learning, making it an essential aspect of an ADHD-friendly space.

Strategies to encourage movement:

- **Accessible Outdoor Space.** Ensure your child has easy access to outdoor spaces. Setting up a mini playground or a basketball hoop can be great if you have a yard. For apartment dwellers, try to find a nearby park where your child can run and play regularly.

- **Active Tools.** Consider using tools that allow movement, like standing desks or fidget toys.
- **Flexible Furnishings.** Consider incorporating furniture that allows or even encourages movement. For example, a standing desk can be adjusted so your child can alternate between sitting and standing. A rocking chair or a swing seat might also offer a calming motion for them.

Noise Level

Every child is different; some may require complete silence for focus, while others might work better with some ambient noise. Try different noise levels and types to see what suits your child best. It could be the hum of a fan, the gentle gurgling of a fish tank, or the soothing notes of instrumental music.

The goal is to find a sound environment that supports rather than disrupts your child's concentration. Remember, what works best for one child may not work for another. The key is to be patient, experiment, and find the perfect balance for your child.

Techniques to ensure silence:

- **Minimize Distractions.** Take stock of your home and identify noise sources that can be controlled. It could be the volume of the TV, the noise of household appliances, or even loud conversations. Minimizing these distractions can help create a calmer, quieter environment.
- **Create a Sound Barrier.** Consider using sound barriers if the noise cannot be controlled—say, you live on a busy street. Using heavy curtains, rugs, or bookshelves filled with books helps absorb and minimize noise from outside.
- **Consider a White Noise Machine.** For some children with ADHD, constant, predictable noise can be calming.

A white noise machine or a fan can provide a steady hum that helps mask other unpredictable, distracting noises.

Sensory Needs of Children with ADHD

Perhaps, in your journey in parenting a child with ADHD, you often come across the term *'sensory needs.' But what exactly are these sensory needs, and why are they so important in an ADHD-friendly environment?*

Having ADHD does not just affect a child's ability to focus or sit still. It can also influence how they experience the world through their senses. Some children with ADHD might be hypersensitive, finding certain sounds disturbing or clothing tags too scratchy. Others might be hyposensitive, craving intense sensory experiences like jumping off swings or blasting music.

There are five commonly known senses: *sight, hearing, touch, taste, and smell.* Yet two lesser-known ones are also crucial: **the vestibular sense (balance and movement)** and **the proprioceptive sense (body awareness).** Children with ADHD may have needs associated with any or all of these senses. By tuning into your child's behaviors and preferences, you can start to understand their sensory profile.

Making an ADHD-friendly Sensory Environment

Here are some sensory strategies you might consider:

Visual Needs

Consider adopting a minimalist approach with neutral colors. However, a spot of personalized decoration or color can also make the space inviting. A visual schedule with pictures or written activities can also provide structure and predictability.

Auditory Needs

As mentioned earlier, create a quieter environment, but also consider the sounds your child may find calming. Some children respond well to white noise machines or soft music. Others might need complete silence during certain tasks.

Tactile Needs

Consider incorporating a variety of textures into your child's environment. A fuzzy rug, a smooth, cool tabletop, or a squishy stress ball can all provide important tactile input. If your child finds certain clothing textures bothersome, choose soft, tagless clothes whenever possible.

Taste and Smell Needs

Pay attention to any preferences your child has regarding foods or smells. Some children might seek strong flavors or scents, while others are more comfortable with bland, predictable sensory input. Respecting these preferences can contribute to a more calming environment.

Vestibular and Proprioceptive Needs

Providing opportunities for movement can help meet vestibular and proprioceptive needs. This might look like frequent breaks for physical activity, a rocking chair for gentle movement, or a weighted blanket for deep pressure. If your child enjoys spinning or jumping, a small trampoline or swing can be a great addition to your home.

Empowering through Sensory Strategies

Understanding your child's sensory needs is not just about minimizing challenges but also about empowering them. For instance, if your child is hypersensitive to noise, teaching them to use headphones or retreat to a quiet space can greatly help. When your child craves intense movement, getting them involved in sports or dance can positively channel this need.

Remember, understanding your child's sensory needs is a journey, not a destination. Be ready to adapt and change your strategies as your child grows and their needs shift. Create an environment where your child feels understood and supported in their unique sensory experience.

Setting Clear Rules and Expectations

Like physical spaces, behavioral environments shape a child's development. Clear rules and expectations act as the framework of this environment. They help the child understand what is expected of them, provide consistency, and promote safety and predictability. These aspects can be especially beneficial for children with ADHD, who may struggle with impulsivity, inattention, and hyperactivity.

Think of rules and expectations as a guide to your child's behavior. Like lines on a road, rules provide direction and reduce uncertainty and confusion. This helps relieve some of the stress and anxiety ADHD children can feel. For example, a rule like *"Homework first, TV later"* clearly defines what to do.

Creating a Framework of Rules

When setting rules, ensure they are—

- **Specific.** A rule needs to be as specific as possible. For instance, instead of saying, *"Be good,"* you might say, *"Use your inside voice when you are in the house."*
- **Simple.** Remember to keep these rules simple and digestible. Children with ADHD may find it challenging to remember or adhere to a rule that is too complex or has too many parts. The aim is to make it as easy for your child to comprehend what is expected of them as possible.
- **Concrete.** Rules should be about tangible behaviors you can see, and your child can control. Instead of *"Be respectful,"* a more concrete rule could be, *"When someone is speaking, wait your turn before you start talking."*

Take the time to explain these rules to your child. But do not just tell them the rules; help them understand why they are necessary.

Clarifying Expectations

Rules provide a *"what"* to do or not do. Meanwhile, expectations set the *"how."* These expectations dictate how your child should behave in specific situations, emphasizing behavior, effort, and responsibility. For example, an expectation could be, *"When you come home from school, your backpack must be emptied, and your homework is placed on your desk."* This guides your child's behavior and also specifies the effort required.

While setting expectations, bear in mind your child's abilities and age. If the bar is set too high, it can lead to frustration and a sense of inadequacy, while setting it too low may not provide enough of a challenge to stimulate growth and development.

Consistency and Involvement in Rules and Expectations

Constantly changing or inconsistently enforcing rules can lead to confusion, making it harder for your child to follow them. If a rule is established, it needs to be consistently followed through.

Involve also your child in this process. Children are more likely to follow the rules they have participated in creating. Doing so will give them a sense of control and aid in better understanding the rules themselves.

Importance of Consequences and Rewards

When establishing rules, also clarify the consequences of breaking them and the rewards for following them.

For example, let your child know that if they do not put their toys away after playing, they cannot play with them the next day. This consequence, directly linked to the rule, is not overly punitive but educational, showing the child the natural outcome of not tidying up.

Rewards can motivate your child to follow the rules. Remember, rewards need not be extravagant. A simple word of praise, an additional 10 minutes of playtime, or the privilege to pick the family movie can be effective rewards. Ensure that you consistently implement these rewards when your child adheres to the rules.

Chapter 5
Routines and Consistency

Having a routine and being consistent helps your child navigate daily life. Encompassing this chapter are the benefits of creating a routine. Likewise, practical strategies to help establish and maintain daily routines will be shared.

But since we live in an unpredictable world, making things go as planned, this chapter will also discuss flexibility in routines. After all, the aim is not to create a rigid structure but to build a fluid, dynamic routine that supports your child's development while accommodating life's unpredictability.

Benefits of Consistent Routines

Consistent schedules and structure every day help children thrive. These give stability, predictability, and a feeling of control, which helps kids who struggle with executive function challenges like organization and focus. At first, sticking to a routine may be hard. But over time, it becomes an indispensable tool to reduce stress and improve concentration.

Some other benefits of a consistent routine include the following:

Establishes Healthy Habits

Following set routines day after day helps promote healthy habits in children with ADHD. For example, consistent wake-up times and bedtimes ensure children get adequate sleep, which is linked to improved concentration and behaviors.

Brushing teeth, eating meals, completing homework, and getting ready for bed are all important tasks that children will come to expect and be prepared for. Routines allow these essential activities to become ingrained, automatic behaviors. With this, important self-care tasks also become habits rather than daily struggles.

Boosts Focus and Productivity

Children with ADHD often struggle to stay on task and manage their time effectively. Routines provide the structure that can account for these challenges. When activities are performed in the same order daily, children no longer have to exert as much mental energy figuring out what they should be doing.

These reduce distractions and time wasted deciding what to do next. Also, children with set schedules can focus on the expected task. Thus, daily routines promote organization by designating specific times for homework, play, chores, etc., and help children make the most of their time and energy.

Reduces Morning and Evening Disorders

Mornings and bedtimes are peak times of chaos in households with children with ADHD. Without structure, mornings can quickly devolve into last-minute crises over missing homework, shoes, backpacks, and meals. Implementing consistent morning routines with set wake-up times, hygiene checklists, and prepared backpacks the night before leads to smoother, less frazzled mornings.

Additionally, strict nightly routines are essential for ensuring children get enough sleep, which can be especially challenging if other behavioral disorders accompany ADHD. Establishing a consistent evening wind-down routine helps avoid these bedtime battles.

Provides Comfort through Predictability

The structure of daily routines enables ADHD children to regulate themselves. Instead of constant parental reminders, the familiar schedules become organizational aids. Over time, following structured routines becomes natural and even comforting. ADHD kids feel confidently in control when predictable routines guide them through each day. It gives them an idea of what to expect. This reduces anxiety since there are no surprises to trigger their symptoms.

Improves Cooperation and Compliance

With time, consistent routines become accepted rules for ADHD kids rather than things they fight about. When activities happen regularly, children learn to cooperate instead of resist. For instance, if homework time is after school every day, kids start to expect and prepare for it.

Strengthens Family Relationships

Families grow closer through sharing fixed routines day after day. Children learn to trust and depend on set family guidelines when parents establish age-appropriate routines and enforce them calmly. Smoothly running routines demonstrate that parents are in control and can be counted on to meet children's basic needs.

Strategies for Daily Routines

A daily routine is not just about prescribing a set of tasks for your child to follow. It is also not just about creating a strict timetable that your child must follow to the minute. Instead, it is about creating a structured sequence of activities that organizes your child's day, providing predictability and reducing uncertainty.

Typically, a daily routine includes activities from when your child wakes up through school hours until they wind down for sleep. The tasks include hygiene practices, meal times, schoolwork, playtime, and other personal or family responsibilities.

However, remember to consider your child's unique needs and preferences while laying out these tasks. For example, if your child is not a morning person, scheduling important tasks or activities requiring intense focus in the morning might not work well. Instead, align the routine to their natural rhythms. This tailoring of the routine makes it more achievable and less of a burden for your child and contributes to their overall motivation to adhere to it.

Tips When Creating and Implementing Routines

Below are strategies you can use to create and maintain routines. With these strategies in hand, you are setting a routine and your child up for a life of learning, growing, and thriving.

Break It Down

When faced with a large, complex project, the most effective approach is to break it down into smaller, more manageable tasks. This strategy, often called *"chunking,"* applies perfectly when establishing a routine for your child with ADHD.

To start, divide the day into broad segments: *morning, school time, after-school, and evening*. Then, within these blocks, delineate specific activities. For example, the morning block could consist of tasks like waking up, getting dressed, brushing teeth, having breakfast, and preparing for school.

Consistent Sleep Schedule

Adequate, quality sleep is essential for all children. Poor sleep can exacerbate ADHD symptoms, making it more difficult for children to focus and manage emotions. Therefore, establishing a consistent sleep schedule is integral to your child's daily routine.

Ensure your child gets into bed and wakes up at the same time every day, even on weekends. This regularity helps their body clock establish a stable sleep-wake rhythm. Begin the bedtime routine about an hour before your child's designated sleep time to help them wind down. This routine could include bathing, reading a story, or some other calming activity that signals the brain that it is time to sleep.

Create Visual Aids

Visual aids are an excellent tool for helping children with ADHD follow their daily routines. These aids can be anything from a simple hand-drawn chart to a colorful poster or digital app. The main goal is to provide your child with a clear, visible representation of their daily routine that they can easily refer to.

Place these visual aids in a conspicuous location that your child frequents. For example, a morning routine chart could be placed on the bathroom mirror or the refrigerator door. Include pictures along with the words, especially for younger children, as it makes the routine more engaging and easier to understand. The visual aid will help remind your kid of the tasks ahead and help reduce the need for constant parental supervision.

Factor in Downtime

Continuous activity without breaks can lead to frustration and burnout, reducing the overall effectiveness of the routine. Incorporating periods of relaxation or free time into the routine can help your child recharge and manage their energy levels more effectively.

Downtime does not necessarily mean doing nothing. It can involve unstructured play, a short walk, listening to music, or daydreaming on the bed. The point is to provide an opportunity for your child to step away from the routine and relax.

Active Time

Include periods of active time within your child's daily routine. Exercise and physical activity can help manage ADHD symptoms as these burn off excess energy, improve mood, and enhance concentration. Active time can take different forms based on your child's preferences. It could be a morning run around the block, an afternoon soccer practice, or an evening bike ride.

Homework Strategies

Doing homework requires sustained focus and sitting still, which is typically challenging for children diagnosed with ADHD. But to make it manageable, break homework time into smaller segments with short breaks in between. This approach, known as the ***Pomodoro Technique,*** can help prevent burnout and maintain focus.

Besides that, create a conducive environment for homework. This could mean a quiet, well-lit corner of the house, free from distractions. Lastly, ensure your child has all the necessary materials before starting their work to reduce interruptions.

Involve Your Child

Developing a routine is not something you should do alone. Involve your child in the process. Discuss with them the purpose of having a routine and how it can help them.

Start by having an open discussion about what tasks need to be included in the daily routine. Then, allow them to choose when they prefer to do certain tasks. This could mean deciding whether to do homework before or after their active time.

Make a balance between providing structure and allowing flexibility so your child feels a part of the process and not just a passive participant.

Regular Check-Ins

Review and adjust the routine based on your child's changing needs and feedback. As they grow older, their activities, responsibilities, and even their ADHD symptoms may evolve, which means the routine needs to adapt as well.

Use these check-ins to discuss what is working and what is not with your child. Ask if they have enough downtime, if the homework strategy is effective, or if they are struggling with a particular task. Regular reviews keep the routine dynamic and responsive, ensuring it continues to serve your child's needs effectively.

Celebrate Success

Remember to celebrate your child's success, no matter how small. Positive reinforcement encourages continued adherence to the routine and boosts your child's self-esteem.

Mark milestones like six months or a year of consistency. This helps families appreciate progress and motivates further success. At monthly or annual markers, share favorite memories, remember how far routines have come, express gratitude, and enjoy special treats.

The Ongoing Challenge of Maintaining Routines with ADHD

No matter how well-designed, routines require upkeep and commitment. As children grow and life gets busy, even the best routines can falter without watchful maintenance. Below are tips and strategies for upholding effective routines through the constantly shifting challenges of raising a child with ADHD.

Reinforcing Routines through Repetition

The magic of routines lies in repetitive consistency over an extended timeframe. At first, routines feel new, strange, or even oppressive. But through daily repetition, they become automatic and reassuring.

Maintaining routines means powering through the adjustment period until desired habits become embedded. For children with ADHD who struggle with transitions, change, and self-regulation, this process may take longer than usual. Consistency, positivity, and perseverance are necessary.

With time and practice, new routines transform from oddities into indispensable life rafts children cling to for stability.

Tuning Routines as Needed

Over time, routines may require tweaking and adjustments to keep working optimally. Children may resist parental control over routines as they mature, especially regarding bedtime, technology use, homework, and chores. Maintaining compliance requires a change in approach.

Involve children in updating routines to fit changing needs. Be open to negotiation within limits. Explain the reasons behind routines again and allow some flexibility in scheduling. Provide increased autonomy wherever possible. Stay patient, firm, and consistent in upholding family routines with empathy as children test boundaries.

Recommitting After Lapses

Remember, fallbacks are part of progress for ADHD families. Children may have setbacks in behavior, and parents may lapse in enforcing routines for periods, especially due to stressors like holidays or illnesses.

Reset and firmly recommit to re-establishing lapsed routines without shaming or dwelling on past issues. Children should not sense lingering disappointments. Move forward with optimism and a clean slate. Consistency may take time to regain, but it is doable.

Flexibility in Routines

Consistency is a pillar of an effective routine, as is flexibility. There will be days when things do not go as planned, which is alright. Instead of rigidly adhering to the routine at the cost of your child's well-being, be willing to make adjustments as needed.

While structure is essential, some flexibility can also be built into routines. Setting times for homework, play, and meals is helpful, but the order can be switched around occasionally based on needs.

For instance, if your child has had a particularly challenging day at school, they might benefit from extra downtime rather than diving straight into homework. Or if they have had a poor night's sleep, they might need a quieter day with fewer tasks.

Flexibility helps cater the routine to real life, demonstrating to your child that while routines provide structure, they are not unyielding rules.

Some tips for handling disruptions to routines with flexibility include the following:

- **Have substitute routines ready for sick days, snow days, or holidays.** Doing so will help kids handle schedule deviations smoothly. For example, have a standard sick day routine with favorite movies, books, and comfort foods.
- **Establish travel routines for maintaining consistency in new environments like hotels or relatives' houses.** Pack familiar items like favorite pajamas or books. Stick to normal bedtime routines.
- **Focus on getting back on track after disruptions rather than demanding perfection.** Praise flexibility and adaptations.
- **Allow some flexibility within the routine sometimes.** Switch around homework to play time orders based on your child's needs that day.
- **Build extra downtime or quiet time when your child seems stressed or overtired.** Adjust activities to match their state.
- **Bend routine when necessary.** Remember, the goal is a fluid routine that meets your child's needs—not a rigid schedule.
- **Accept that unforeseen events will sometimes force you to modify routines.** Do not sweat small bumps; aim to minimize disruption.
- **When plans change, explain it simply to your child.** Ease uncertainty by outlining the new routine and giving warnings of transitions.
- **Stay calm, supportive, and flexible when disruptions occur.** Your child will learn to adapt. Maintain routines as much as realistically possible.

Chapter 6
Positive Reinforcement

Sometimes, to get a child to follow the rules or do chores, parents give them ultimatums. Yet, a proven way exists to motivate kids with ADHD without threats or bribes. Such a method is called *positive reinforcement.* This refers to rewarding good behavior, which can change problematic behaviors when used consistently.

In this chapter, you will learn more about what positive reinforcement is. Likewise, understand how to use it to improve your child's behavior. Different reward types, which give different effects, will also be covered. Lastly, this chapter will address reward-related challenges and how to resolve them.

Role of Positive Reinforcement

Envision a trainer training a dog. Every time the dog does tricks at the trainer's command, it will be rewarded with a treat. When the trainer always does this, *what do you think happens?* Likely, the dog will do more tricks because it will receive a delicious reward. Such a situation is the basis of positive reinforcement.

Positive reinforcement is widely used in psychology and behavioral therapy, which emphasizes rewarding desired behaviors. Applying positive reinforcement to children, especially those with ADHD, is not as straightforward as giving treats to a dog. But at its core, positive reinforcement means recognizing and rewarding a child's desirable behaviors, encouraging them to repeat such actions in the future.

To help you better understand the power of this approach in parenting, the benefits of applying positive reinforcement are listed below.

Encourages Good Behavior

Children, especially those with ADHD, often need external motivation to behave in a desired way. Positive reinforcement provides this motivation. For example, let us say your child has difficulty focusing on homework. To encourage concentration, you could introduce a reward system: *for every 15 minutes of uninterrupted homework, they earn a 5-minute break to do something they enjoy.* This reward system acts as a motivator, nudging them towards focusing on their tasks.

Builds Confidence

For children with ADHD, tasks that may seem simple to others, like focusing on homework for 10 minutes or sitting still during a family dinner, can be significant challenges. They often receive feedback about what they are doing wrong, leading to feelings of frustration and inadequacy. However, the results can be excellent if you replace this criticism with positive reinforcement.

When you focus on what they are doing right and reward them for it, they begin to see their abilities rather than just their shortcomings. For instance, if your child has ADHD and struggles with homework, instead of saying, *"You are always late with your homework,"* try, *"I noticed you started your homework as soon as you got home today. That is fantastic!"* Such an approach promotes the desired behavior rather than focusing on the negatives.

Nurtures the Parent-Child Relationship

Parenting a child can sometimes feel like a constant cycle of stress and conflict. Positive reinforcement can help break this cycle. As stated earlier, when you engage in positive reinforcement, you actively focus on your child's good behaviors and efforts rather than their shortcomings. This shift in perspective can foster a more positive and supportive parent-child relationship.

Imagine this: Instead of constantly scolding your child for leaving their toys scattered, you praise them each time they put a toy away. Over time, your child will likely start putting away their toys more frequently, eager for your praise. Not only does this promote good behavior, but it also encourages positive interactions between you and your child.

Employing Positive Reinforcement

Below are practical tips and techniques to help you incorporate positive reinforcement into your parenting strategy.

Start with Clear Expectations

Before employing positive reinforcement, define the behaviors you want to encourage in your child. Be specific. Instead of saying, *"Behave well,"* specify what 'good behavior' entails, like *"Sit quietly while doing homework"* or *"Put your toys away after playtime."* Clear expectations give your child a solid understanding of what they should aim for.

Choose Meaningful Rewards

Rewards are the heart of positive reinforcement. Choosing rewards your child will genuinely value and desire is essential. These can vary from child to child. One might value extra playtime, while another might love a special treat or privilege. Do not limit yourself to material rewards. Remember, a simple hug or words of praise can be just as meaningful.

Immediate Reinforcement

Reward your child immediately after they exhibit the desired behavior. This immediate feedback helps them associate the reward with the specific behavior, reinforcing it. For instance, if your child completes their homework without distraction, praise them or immediately give the promised reward. Do not wait so your child does not lose interest. This helps strengthen the connection between the desired behavior and the positive reinforcement.

Use a Reward System

Consider using a reward system to make positive reinforcement more systematic and consistent. This could be a sticker chart, a token system, or an earned privileges system. For example, when your child completes a desired behavior, they earn a sticker. Accumulated stickers can be exchanged for a larger reward, such as a family outing.

Be Consistent

Consistency is key in positive reinforcement. The more consistent you are with rewarding desired behaviors, the more likely your child is to repeat those behaviors. Ensure that all caregivers involved with your child *(like teachers or babysitters)* understand and follow your reinforcement strategies.

Balance with Natural Consequences

While positive reinforcement is about rewarding good behaviors, still let your child face the natural consequences of inappropriate behaviors. This balance helps your child understand that while good behaviors have positive outcomes, inappropriate behaviors have less desirable ones.

Avoid Bribery

Know the difference between positive reinforcement and bribery. *Bribery* often involves giving rewards upfront to control behavior, which can lead to a lack of internal motivation. *Positive reinforcement*, on the other hand, rewards behaviors after they happen, encouraging your child to repeat them for the right reasons.

Praise Effort Over Outcome

Remember to focus on the effort your child is making rather than the outcome. Praise them for trying, for improving, for persisting. This reinforces a growth mindset, teaching your child that effort and persistence are as crucial as the result.

Be Patient

Changes in behavior take time. Celebrate small victories, and do not get disheartened if progress seems slow. With consistent positive reinforcement, your child will gradually adopt the desired behaviors.

Different Reward Types

There are various types of rewards, and each can impact children with ADHD differently.

Tangible Rewards

Tangible rewards are physical items or actions a child can see, touch, or experience directly. Examples include *toys, favorite food items, or outings to a cherished place like a park.*

For instance, visualize your child completing their homework without any reminders or assistance. Rewarding them with their favorite comic book can be a powerful motivator for them to repeat the behavior in the future.

However, tread carefully with tangible rewards. Overuse can lead to a situation where the child performs tasks only to receive the reward, not because they understand the importance of the task itself. Balance tangible rewards with other reward types for more holistic motivation and growth.

Intangible Rewards

Intangible rewards are non-physical forms of rewards that are equally important. These can be in *praise, recognition, or expressions of love and affection.*

Continuing our example of the homework task, an intangible reward might be a hug, a heartfelt *"Well done!"* or a special note of appreciation. These rewards can help a child with ADHD feel a sense of achievement, bolster their self-esteem, and create a positive association with the task at hand.

Remember, children with ADHD often struggle with feelings of inadequacy and failure. The power of positive words and emotions can make a significant difference in their motivation levels.

Social Rewards

Social rewards are centered on the social aspect of the reward experience. They are intended to fulfill a child's need for social interaction, acceptance, and belonging. These rewards involve interactions with other people, such as *family game nights, a playdate with a best friend, or even extra time to chat with grandparents over a video call.*

Assume your child has been working hard at managing their symptoms. A great social reward might be inviting their friends over for a sleepover. Such rewards provide fun and a chance to practice social skills in a safe environment.

Activity Rewards

Activity rewards are enjoyable activities that your child loves to engage in. This could be anything from *extra playtime, a bike ride, an art session, or time spent playing a favorite video game.*

Suppose your child has been showing progress in controlling impulsive behavior. In that case, an activity reward could be allowing them to choose the family movie for the evening or deciding the menu for dinner.

Privilege Rewards

Privilege rewards involve granting your child certain privileges or benefits they would not typically have. This could range from *staying up a little later on a weekend, choosing the family outing spot, or even being allowed to have dessert before dinner.*

As a parent, you have the authority to grant these privileges, and when used correctly, they can act as powerful motivators for your child to demonstrate desirable behaviors.

Choosing the Right Reward

After exploring the different types of rewards, the question arises—*which is the best for your child with ADHD?* The answer lies in knowing your child's preferences, what motivates them, and what aligns with your family's values and resources.

A good starting point is to have an open conversation with your child about what they consider a reward. Incorporate a variety of reward types and observe which ones resonate most with your child. The goal is to help your child feel motivated, validated, and excited to continue their progress.

Remember, rewards do not always have to be big or grand. Often, small, consistent rewards have the most significant impact.

Addressing Reward-Related Challenges

One of the first steps in addressing reward-related challenges is understanding them. There are many potential pitfalls when using rewards for positive reinforcement. These include:

Shallow Understanding of Desired Behavior

When children receive rewards only for a result, they might not understand the value of the process or the behavior leading to it. This can create a mindset where they merely chase the reward instead of genuinely understanding and appreciating the behavior's inherent benefits.

Alongside the reward, explain the value of the behavior. For instance, if a child finishes a book and gets rewarded, take the time to discuss what they learned from the story. This way, they associate the reward with the outcome and the process.

Diminishing Effects

Over time, the same reward might lose its charm. If a child gets the same treat every time they complete a task, they might grow bored or expectant of it, diminishing its effectiveness as positive reinforcement.

Periodically review and adjust the rewards. Offer variety or occasionally upgrade the rewards to keep them enticing. Moreover, periodically ask your child about rewards they might find motivating, ensuring their preferences guide the reward system.

Unrealistic Expectations

When children expect a reward for every good behavior or action, they may develop a sense of entitlement or grow frustrated when rewards are not forthcoming in other settings, like at school or a friend's house.

Set clear boundaries around when and why rewards are given. Ensure the child understands that while rewarded for specific behaviors at home, the same might not always apply elsewhere. This is an opportunity to discuss the inherent value of good behavior, regardless of external rewards.

Neglect of Non-tangible Rewards

Physical rewards can sometimes overshadow non-tangible rewards like verbal praise or quality time, which are equally *(if not more)* effective.

Integrate a mix of tangible and non-tangible rewards. Alongside a toy or treat, invest time in activities the child loves. For example, if they have been helpful around the house, a day out in the park or a special movie night can be a rewarding experience that strengthens bonds.

Dependency

If rewards are always expected, children might grow dependent on them and not act without a reward's promise.

Gradually reduce the frequency of rewards as the desired behavior becomes habitual. The goal is to make the behavior a natural part of the child's routine without needing external motivation.

By being mindful of these pitfalls and actively working to address them, rewards can help encourage and sustain positive behaviors in children.

Exercise: Practicing Positive Reinforcement

This exercise outlines how to enforce simple positive reinforcement that communicates your expectations. In just one week of practice, you will see the power of positive reinforcement in action. And you will gain first-hand experience using this approach that you can continue to implement long-term. This positive reinforcement exercise will help motivate your child and make parenting more enjoyable.

Instructions:

1. **Choose One to Three Specific Behaviors.** Decide what behaviors you want to reinforce. These could include basic habits like making their bed, brushing their teeth, or putting toys away. Or they could be skills you are actively trying to build, like waiting patiently, following instructions, or controlling emotions.
2. **Consistently Notice and Praise Positive Behaviors.** While generic praise like *"good job"* can have unintended consequences, such as reducing a child's intrinsic motivation, it's still important to encourage them. When you see your child demonstrating the target behaviors, immediately praise them. Instead of relying heavily on general affirmations, focus on acknowledging the effort your child put into their task or comment on specific actions they did well. This fosters a sense of accomplishment and encourages them to continue the behavior. For instance, instead of saying, *"Good job,"* you could say, *"You were patient while waiting your turn."*

3. **Provide Meaningful Rewards.** After praising them, give a small reward to reinforce the behavior. Make sure rewards are motivating to your child. Vary them to keep it exciting.
4. **Track Progress with a Chart.** Use a chart, stickers, or points to let your child see their positive behaviors accumulating.
5. **Stay Positive.** Gently remind them if they forget a behavior. Harsh criticism undermines motivation. Progress takes time, so stick with it.
6. **Check-In and Tweak as Needed.** After a week, check in with your child. Adjust your rewards and system based on their input.
7. **Practice Consistently.** With consistency, positive behaviors will increase. You can introduce new behaviors to target once the first reinforced behavior sticks to the child.
8. **Reduce Rewards Gradually.** Eventually, you can reduce external rewards as behaviors become habits.

Chapter 7
Effective Communication

Communication is the lifeline of any relationship. With a child who has ADHD, there can be times when you feel lost in translation. Misunderstandings arise, and conversations feel one-sided. But do not lose heart; every interaction is a chance to improve how you relate to your child.

The importance of open communication will be discussed in this chapter. Unravel also the strategies for understanding and empathy. As well as the art of delivering clear instructions.

Understanding Open Communication

In parenting, communication is often seen as a two-way street. Both parents and children have the right to share advice, set boundaries, and voice their opinions. With ADHD, maintaining this two-way communication can be challenging. Children may struggle with listening, concentration, or impulsivity, making it harder to absorb and respond to your messages effectively.

Open communication delves deeper into this exchange as verbal and non-verbal cues are crucial and can offer a more holistic approach to these interactions. It is not just about issuing instructions or making requests. Rather, it is about going beyond the traditional directive-response model of communication. Through this, you connect with your child and understand their feelings, needs, thoughts, inner experiences and perspectives.

Factors That Impact Communication

Children with ADHD face distinct challenges that profoundly influence their communication abilities. Here are some of the most common challenges that can affect how you communicate with your child:

- **Impulsiveness.** Affects communication by leading to frequent interruptions and comments made without thinking first.
- **Inattention.** Children with ADHD have shortened attention spans, making concentrating during lengthy or complex dialogues hard. Kids may seem distracted or disengaged. Multi-step instructions are challenging to absorb fully.
- **Hyperactivity.** Hyperactivity causes restlessness during sit-down conversations. Sitting still requires great effort, impacting the ability to listen closely throughout an entire discussion.
- **Emotional dysregulation.** This means feelings become overwhelming easily. Big emotions like anger, excitement, or frustration interfere with the capacity to communicate calmly. Meltdowns shut down productive communication.

Importance to Parent-Children Relationships

Open communication stands as the pillar of trust in a parent-child relationship. It *nurtures an environment where children feel safe to express their thoughts and feelings without fear of judgment or criticism.* Children with ADHD often struggle with expressing themselves effectively. They might exhibit feelings of frustration, anger, or sadness in ways that might seem excessive or inappropriate.

When parents employ open communication, they can *decode these emotional outbursts.* For instance, your child with ADHD suddenly seems frustrated and angrily kicks a toy. Instead of immediately reprimanding or dismissing the action as *"just another outburst,"* practicing open communication would involve approaching the child calmly and asking, *"I noticed you seemed upset when you kicked the toy. Do you want to talk about what's bothering you?"* This approach avoids immediate judgment and allows the child to express themselves.

Doing so **bridges the gap of misunderstanding**, creating a bond of trust where the child feels valued and heard. It also instills a sense of security in the child, making them more likely to approach their parents with problems or concerns. As parents become attuned to their children's emotions and struggles, they can offer more tailored guidance and support, decreasing frustration and conflicts at home. Furthermore, children who feel understood are more likely to develop positive self-esteem, resilience, and coping skills.

Practical Approaches to Fostering Open Communication

Fostering open communication with your child is an ongoing process that requires dedication and care. An atmosphere of understanding does not happen overnight—it needs consistent nurturing through mindful communication habits. While it takes time and effort, the rewards of deeper mutual understanding between parent and child are invaluable.

Below are some tips to help lay the groundwork for open communication in your parenting.

1. **Active Listening.** Active listening is more than just hearing the words your child says. It involves fully engaging with them, showing empathy, and consciously trying to understand their point of view.

To practice active listening, do the following:

- ***Be fully present.*** Set aside your phone, stop what you are doing, and give your child your attention. This shows them that you value what they say.
- ***Reflect and validate.*** After your child has spoken, paraphrase their words to show you understand. For instance, if they are upset about a school incident, you could say, *"It sounds like you had a tough day. That must have been really hard for you."* This validates their feelings and encourages them to share more.

2. **Nonverbal Communication.** Nonverbal communication, such as body language, facial expressions, and behavior, can provide important insights into children's feelings. Since ADHD can make it difficult for children to verbally express their emotions, their nonverbal cues may reveal inner states that they struggle to articulate in words alone. However, the meaning behind these cues is complex and depends on context. While they should be considered, they do not always speak louder than words for children with ADHD. Careful verbal and nonverbal communication interpretation is needed to understand their perspectives and emotions fully.

Here are ways you can tune in to nonverbal communication:

- ***Observe body language.*** Look for changes in your child's posture, facial expressions, or movements. *Are they crossing their arms defensively? Are their faces showing signs of stress or upset?*
- ***Listen to the tone.*** Even if the words seem neutral, a change in tone can signal a shift in mood or emotional state. *Is their voice tense, shaky, or louder than usual?*

3. **Encourage Expression.** Encouraging your child to express their feelings can give them the push they need to communicate effectively.

    Do the following:

    - *Use creative outlets.* Provide materials for drawing, painting, or craftwork. These activities allow children to express their feelings visually and can provide a talking point for discussing their emotions.
    - *Engage in role-play.* Playing with dolls, puppets, or figurines can help your child explore different situations and emotions in a safe, comfortable setting.

4. **Be a Role Model.** Kids learn how to communicate by observing you. If you show them that you practice open communication, it sets a standard for them to follow.

    Some ways to become a good role model include:

    - *Share your feelings.* Speak openly about your feelings in an age-appropriate manner. Use words and explanations your child can understand based on age and development level. For instance, when speaking with a toddler, say, *"Mommy is sad."* While for a preschooler, you can say, *"Mommy feels disappointed that we cannot go to the park today."*
    - *Apologize when wrong.* If you make a mistake, apologize to your child. This shows them it is acceptable to be wrong and that taking responsibility is important.
    - *Display empathy.* Show empathy when interacting with others. This could be as simple as expressing concern when someone is upset or acknowledging someone else's point of view during a disagreement.

Strategies for Understanding and Empathy

Every step towards empathetic communication is towards a stronger, more trusting relationship with your child. And that is a reward worth striving for.

In being empathetic, acknowledge that your child's experience is unique, challenging, and sometimes incomprehensible to those without ADHD. So, *how can you embed these elements into your everyday communication?* Here are some tips and techniques.

See from Your Child's Perspective

ADHD manifests differently in every child, but fundamentally it impacts how they perceive, interpret, and interact with the world around them. For you as a parent, the behaviors of ADHD can seem baffling, defiant, or intentionally disruptive. But when you make a conscious effort to see from their perspective, you can start to understand the real drivers behind their actions.

A key perspective shift is to understand how ADHD impacts their daily life and experiences. Consider how hard it must be to sit still, resist distractions, focus for sustained periods, switch tasks, remember details, manage time, curb impulses, and organize obligations. The world is an overwhelming and highly stimulating place for a child with ADHD. Sensory input, distractions, and demands are coming at them constantly in school, at home, and in social settings. Imagine navigating all those challenges while being expected to self-regulate at the level of other children; *that is what your child experiences.*

Respecting how your children experience day-to-day life differently helps you reframe behaviors often viewed as defiance or intentional disruption. But to make this shift, you must first walk in their shoes, see the world through their eyes, and understand their hidden struggles.

To understand your child's perspective, do the following:

- Observe them closely to identify pain points and challenges
- Discuss how ADHD makes them feel and what situations are hard
- Imagine yourself with ADHD—*how would you cope? What would help?*
- Reframe behaviors through an ADHD lens
- Give the benefit of the doubt rather than assuming intent

Fundamentally, it requires choosing compassion over frustration or judgment. Understanding rather than control. Patience rather than urgency. This fosters an environment where they feel accepted despite the ways ADHD might manifest. One that makes space for processing and expression. And one where you can partner together to find coping strategies.

The more you see from their perspective, the better you can empathize, support, and solve problems collaboratively. Walking in their shoes breeds understanding. And understanding is the root of effective communication.

Connect Before Correcting

As parents, it is natural to want to correct your children's challenging behaviors. But when parenting a child with ADHD, leading with correction can be counterproductive and strain the parent-child relationship. A better strategy is to connect emotionally first and then address issues from a place of understanding.

The priorities are, in order: *connect, understand, then guide.* A genuine emotional connection must come before attempting to discipline, teach, or change behavior.

Why? Because connection builds trust, rapport, and shared understanding. Children with ADHD often feel misunderstood, criticized, and isolated. Lead with empathy, and you become an ally rather than an adversary. Only once your child feels safely connected can growth occur.

So, *what does connecting look like in practice?*

- **Doing Shared Activities.** Make time for play, creativity projects, being silly, and having fun together. The actual activity does not matter. What matters is the sense that you enjoy their company.
- **Giving Physical Affection.** Hugs, back tickles, and sitting close go a long way. Appropriate physical affection makes children feel cared for. For kids with ADHD who can feel isolated, this is hugely important.
- **Minimize correction.** Minimizing correction when there are high tensions, and everyone is upset can help diffuse the situation. However, follow up on the behavior once there is space for thoughtful discussion and guidance.
- **Give Affirmation.** Verbally share what you appreciate about them—*their humor, creativity, and strengths.* Children with ADHD often only hear correction. Affirmation balances this.
- **Provide Solitude and Space.** Do not force interaction. Let them decompress alone in their room if needed. For introverted or highly stimulated kids, solitude can be connected.
- **Have Child-Directed Conversations.** Ask about their interests, friends, and feelings, and let them lead. *Being heard is validating.*

- These strategies aim to build goodwill, trust, and mutual understanding. This provides a strong foundation from which issues can then be addressed successfully.

Help Them Articulate Their Feelings

Big emotions like anger, frustration, disappointment, or anxiety can feel frightening and overwhelming for young children. When they cannot articulate these emotions, their behaviors often reflect the turmoil inside. Tantrums, shouting, crying, withdrawing—these communication attempts must be met with patience, empathy, and language.

Rather than silencing or minimizing their feelings, your job is to help them develop emotional intelligence and literacy. Here is how:

- **Pay attention to context clues.** When your child is having difficulty vocalizing, look for situational cues. *Did something happen at school? With friends? Are they hungry or tired?* These can provide insight into their internal state.
- **Ask open-ended questions to help them dig deeper.** *"What is making you feel this way?" "Did something happen that upset you?"*
- **If they cannot articulate independently, provide feeling word options.** *"It seems you are feeling angry/sad/anxious/disappointed right now. Is that right?"* Offer choices until you help them identify the primary emotion.
- **Expand their emotional vocabulary.** Expose your child to many feeling words: *delighted, frustrated, embarrassed, jealous, lonely, etc.* Use picture books, flashcards, and discussion. Increased vocabulary gives them new tools.
- **Expand understanding around levels of emotions.** Help them understand the difference between disappointed, devastated, irritated, furious, worried, and terrified. Nuance matters.

With your guidance, your child will gain the language tools to narrate their inner world more articulately. Their ability to identify and communicate their feelings will blossom, and they will gain the capacity to express complex emotions that previously overwhelmed them. This is helpful for you to have greater insight into their inner struggles and needs.

Give them Processing Time

For children with ADHD, navigating the pathways between thoughts, feelings, and spoken words is often complex. What comes naturally and instantly to some requires great mental effort and patience for our kids. You need to understand and respect their unique communication pace.

Rather than rushing to fill silent moments, you must learn to embrace these spaces. Silence is not empty or awkward—it is fertile ground where your child can gather strands of thought and weave them carefully into expression.

To practice patience during this processing time for your child, do the following:

- **Unconditionally accept their unique pace.** Never shame them for not being *"quick enough."* Through words and actions, make it clear that you do not expect fast, perfect responses.
- **Learn to find joy in silence.** Silence invites them inward to unlock their voices. Breathe through the moments rather than filling them.
- **Offer processing time before and after speaking.** Give them space to gather thoughts and clarify afterward.
- **Provide sentence starters if needed,** but let them complete the thought at their cadence.

- **If they lose their train of thought, gently guide them once they are ready.** Wait, and do not interrupt.
- **Watch for signs of being overwhelmed and pause conversations immediately.** Make it a safe space.

The Art of Clear Instructions

Children with ADHD have a harder time absorbing multi-step directions or remembering what tasks they are supposed to be doing. As a parent, you can make your instructions more *'ADHD-friendly'* with the following tips:

Simplify

Giving them a long list of tasks all at once can quickly lead children with ADHD to confusion and overwhelmed. However, breaking such tasks into steps will make your instructions easier to absorb.

Start by taking a big request like *"Clean your room"* and divide it into distinct categories. For example, focus on:

1. Clothes
2. Trash
3. Books
4. Bed
5. Toys

Afterward, break those categories into one to two-step tasks. *"Put all dirty clothes in the laundry basket"* is a clear, concrete instruction they can follow without feeling anxious or distracted.

When giving tasks to children, their mental maturity may not always align with their chronological age. A 10-year-old, for example, might process instructions more similarly to a 7-year-old. In such scenarios, breaking tasks down can be highly effective.

Instead of viewing the entirety of *"Clean your room,"* each small accomplished task gives a sense of satisfaction. The feeling of checking steps off their mental list releases dopamine in their developing brains. This motivates them to keep going and complete the next task.

Over time, chaining these small wins together teaches the bigger skill of cleaning. Just be sure not to make your instructions too basic. *"Pick up shirt"* is reasonable for a 3-year-old but may feel belittling to a 10-year-old. Gauge your language based on their maturity level. With practice, these segmented instructions will build confidence and capability.

Demonstrate

Remember that your child's interpretation of a task may differ. Be precise to avoid mismatched expectations. For example, show them exactly what a *"clean room"* looks like. What appears tidy and orderly in your eyes may still look messy to them. Simply telling them to clean their room leaves too much open to interpretation. During your demonstration, be as detailed and precise as possible.

For example, point out areas they may overlook or not think of as dirty, like crumbs on the floor or dust on a shelf. Show them exactly how you want the books organized or how neatly to fold the clothes before putting them away. Demonstrate making the bed with tightly tucked sheets and smoothed edges. The more thorough your demo, the closer your child's execution will match your expectations.

Resist the urge to criticize their process or past performance. Frame your demonstration as a teaching opportunity, not punishment for doing it wrong. Patiently walk them through the ideal step-by-step process as if for the first time. With consistent modeling, your standards for cleanliness will soon align.

Be Concise

Lengthy, multi-clause sentences can muddle meaning and lose their attention. Try to give instructions using the fewest words possible. For example, *"Shoes on"* rather than *"Do not forget to put your shoes on before we go outside."* Or *"Dishes away"* rather than *"Once you finished eating your food, please put your dishes in the dishwasher."*

Fight the urge to remind, plead, or rationalize. Simple, direct phrases like *"Jacket on"* or *"Homework time"* stick better than wordy sentences. If they ask *"Why?"*, briefly explain reasons after giving instructions rather than tacking on long explanations. And remember to pause between statements to allow time for processing.

With concise communication, their brains can parse less verbal information. Key details can shine through without convoluted extras obscuring the message. Consistently framing instructions in focused, minimalistic language will help increase compliance and comprehension over time.

Focus Their Attention

As children with ADHD struggle to concentrate, especially amid distractions, you should gain their full focus and attention before delivering important instructions. Focused attention is like a muscle—it needs to be exercised regularly to grow stronger. Establishing their concentration before instructions helps train them to stay centered, listen actively, and retain information.

To practice this, make eye contact and call their name to draw them in. Have them repeat the instructions to confirm they were listening. Phrases like *"Listen first"* and *"Watch me"* prepare their brains to tune in to essential information.

Eliminate also the potential distractions in the background before speaking. Turn off the TV and put the devices away. Clear away toys, books, or other stimuli that may divert their concentration. If they appear distracted, gently guide their gaze back to you and ask, *"Are you listening?"* in a neutral tone. Wait until you have their eyes and ears before proceeding.

Write It Down

Verbal instructions vanish quickly, but the written word persists. For children, visible references can make instructions clearer and easier to follow.

Post lists, charts, and step-by-step instructions around the house. Put a morning routine checklist by their bedside, an after-school schedule on the fridge, and a rotating chore chart on the wall. Keep instructions simple using images or icons when possible.

Refer back to these tools frequently when reminding them of expectations. The visual aid helps cement concepts and allows them to self-monitor. Writing also caters to visual learners who benefit from seeing instructions on paper.

Try handing them written steps on a card or sticky note for specific tasks. The portability allows them to carry reminders for on-the-go prompts. And they can check off each step as they complete it for a sense of accomplishment.

Displaying instructions also conveys the message that organizational systems are necessary. With everything documented, following directions becomes more intuitive over time.

Set Alerts

External cueing devices are invaluable for children with ADHD who struggle with time and executive functioning. Timers, alarms, smartwatches, and phone alerts all provide auditory or vibrating prompts to stay on track. When the buzzer rings, they can switch tasks or locations without constant parent reminders. Alerts act like an external working memory, freeing up mental energy.

For example, if it is time to start getting ready for school, set a 7:30 AM alarm reminding them to get out of bed. Before transitions like leaving for an appointment, set a 10-minute timer for finishing tasks and putting on shoes and coats. Match morning and bedtime routines to consistent alarms.

Initially, help them program and respond to alerts. Checking in reinforces the behavior. Once the system is established, alerts create structure and independence. Prompts from devices seem less nagging than from parents. Matching tasks to timed cues builds time management abilities.

Chapter 8
Parent-Teacher Collaboration

Parent-teacher relationships can greatly impact how well your child does academically and socially. This chapter has tips on building strong partnerships with your child's teachers and ensuring you are all working toward the same goals.

Building Partnerships Between Home and School

As a parent, you play a role in bridging communication between your child and their school. Building collaborative partnerships with teachers provides critical insight and aligns support for your child's growth. This teamwork can greatly impact their academic thriving and emotional well-being.

Teachers have valuable frontline observations of your child's needs and triumphs in the classroom. At home, you offer unique context about personality, challenges, and goals. Ongoing dialogue bridges these perspectives.

Initiating the Partnership

The parent-teacher relationship starts with you. Reach out early to introduce yourself and discuss your child's ADHD diagnosis. Providing teachers with background on ADHD equips them to understand your child's needs better. Discuss your child's strengths and challenges, preferred learning styles, what works at home, and goals for the school year. When teachers gain insight into your child as an individual, they can become more empathetic allies.

Set the tone that you and your child's teachers are partners with a shared mission—helping your child thrive. Assure them that you want to collaborate, not criticize. Make yourself available as a resource on ADHD-friendly strategies that may help in the classroom. With open minds and good intentions on both sides, you can build trust and rapport.

Keys to Developing Positive Teacher Relationships

Some helpful strategies to foster productive dialogue and collaboration include the following:

- **Convey empathy for the challenges teachers face.** Validate their hard work and express your appreciation.
- **Approach interactions with a friendly, collaborative tone.** Reassure teachers you want to work together.
- **Listen attentively to understand teachers' perspectives.** Ask questions and gather context.
- **Share insights from home to help teachers "get" your child better.** Provide information that promotes empathy.
- When concerns arise, **focus on joint problem-solving** instead of blaming or venting emotions.
- **Thank teachers sincerely** when they implement agreed-upon strategies or show extra effort. Gratitude matters.
- **Seek opportunities to provide positive feedback** about your child's progress, not just discuss problems.
- **Model reliability.** Follow through consistently on your responsibilities and commitments as a parent.

Maintaining Open Communication

Frequent communication with your child's teachers is key for monitoring progress, tackling challenges in real time, and ensuring proper support. Set up systems for regular check-ins through your preferred means like email, text, phone calls, or in-person meetings. Share observations from home, ask for teacher feedback and discuss concerns early before they escalate. Problem-solve together, aligning home and school solutions.

When challenges crop up, remain calm and collaborative. Remember, you and your child's teachers have the same goal. Support teachers in helping your child, and make it clear you appreciate their efforts. With ongoing teamwork and empathy on both sides, you can work through bumps.

Collaborating on School Accommodations

Work with teachers to develop school accommodations that match your child's needs. An ADHD diagnosis may qualify your child for formal support plans like an IEP or 504 plan.

Discuss recommended academic and behavioral modifications. If your child already has an IEP or 504, actively participate in plan reviews. Provide input on which supports are working versus which need to be adjusted. Ensure your child's plan is updated regularly to fit their evolving profile.

Understanding IEPs and 504 Plans

If your child struggles academically or behaviorally due to ADHD, formal support plans can provide helpful, legally mandated accommodations and services. Two common options are Individualized **Education Programs (IEPs)** and **504 plans**. As a parent new to special education, the process may initially be confusing.

Below is an overview of how these plans work.

What is an Education Program (IEP)?

An IEP is a legal document developed by a team including you, teachers, and school professionals outlining specialized instruction and services for a student with a disability who requires them to learn effectively. To qualify for an IEP, your child must undergo an evaluation showing they meet the criteria for one of the 13 disability classifications under special education law. ADHD alone does not automatically qualify a child, but ADHD combined with certain learning or behavioral challenges can.

The IEP outlines customized goals for your child and details the accommodations, modifications, supplemental aids, services, and programming needed to achieve those goals. The team reviews and updates the IEP annually. You can also request revisions at any time. IEP services can include adjustments like reduced workload, extra time on tests, preferential seating, and behavioral support. If required services are not provided, you can take steps to enforce the IEP.

What is a 504 Plan?

A 504 plan refers to ***Section 504 of the Rehabilitation Act***, a civil rights law to eliminate disability discrimination in programs receiving federal funds. Unlike an IEP, a 504 plan does not provide specialized instruction but does mandate reasonable accommodations for students with disabilities.

To qualify for a 504, your child must have a physical or mental impairment substantially limiting a major life activity. *ADHD is considered a disability under Section 504.* The 504 teams will develop a plan detailing accommodations enabling your child to access the standard school program on par with students without disabilities.

For example, accommodations can include reduced homework, use of fidgets, additional time for assignments, and seating near the teacher.

Pursuing an IEP or 504

When you suspect your child needs an IEP or 504 plan, make a written request to evaluate for special education services. The school will gather data, consult teachers, and conduct formal assessments if necessary to determine if your child meets eligibility criteria. But you can also provide private evaluations and pursue this process anytime.

Arriving prepared with records, educating yourself on the law, and advocating assertively while maintaining a cordial tone can help you secure appropriate services and plans for your child. But the most important thing is collaborating as a team to find solutions. With persistence and partnership, you and your child's school can develop a plan tailored to their needs.

At any time, collaborate with teachers on informal accommodations tailored to your child's needs. Find solutions that allow your ADHD child to shine in the classroom.

Advocating for Your Child

As a parent, do not underestimate your role as an advocate, as you know your child best. Politely but firmly request meetings if you have pressing concerns. Come prepared with specific examples and suggestions. If certain supports are needed but the school is resistant, persist calmly. Know your rights and utilize formal procedures if needed, but aim for open dialogue and mutual understanding first. With a solutions-focused approach, you can often get teachers on board.

Maximizing Parent-Teacher Meetings

Parent-teacher conferences are invaluable opportunities to discuss your child's progress, voice concerns, and align support.

Do not hesitate to politely request meetings with teachers at any time to discuss emerging needs, debrief on what is working or not working, modify your child's learning plan, or address concerns. Come prepared with talking points and potential solutions. Bring your child when appropriate so they can add their perspective.

Also, invite other parents who are also going through similar experiences. They can provide invaluable empathy and ideas. Emotional support enables you to avoid burnout and be more confident during school meetings. Here are some tips you can try over the course of the meeting.

Before the meeting:

- Write down your priorities and goals for the discussion. Focus on one to two major issues.
- Prepare relevant notes, records, and examples to provide context on concerns.
- Think through potential solutions and accommodations to suggest.
- Provide teachers with background information to better understand your child.
- Give teachers a heads-up on major issues you want to address.

During the meeting:

- Set a friendly, collaborative tone. Express your desire to work together.
- Share observations and concerns about your child's learning or behavior. Provide details and concrete examples.
- Ask questions and listen actively to understand the teacher's perspective. There may be things you are not aware of.
- Discuss your child's strengths and challenges openly. Highlight areas of improvement.
- Brainstorm accommodations and strategies together. Offer your ideas while inviting teacher input.
- Agree on reasonable next steps and an action plan with specific follow-up dates, dividing responsibilities.
- Voice any pressing concerns assertively yet politely. Steer the discussion cooperatively toward solutions.

After the meeting:

- Review and summarize key discussion points, agreements, and next steps after you leave.
- Share feedback with co-parents or caregivers so you are all aligned.
- Provide positive reinforcement to teachers when agreed-upon strategies are implemented.
- Follow through on action items you committed to. Check-in on progress at scheduled times.
- Request additional meetings to address ongoing concerns, update plans, or modify approaches.

Exercise: Roleplaying a Parent-Teacher Conference

Practicing conferencing skills in a risk-free environment can transform parent-teacher meetings from stressful to successful.

In this roleplaying exercise, you will learn to:

- Initiate dialogue diplomatically
- Voice concerns constructively
- Suggest accommodations collaboratively
- Find shared goals and understanding
- End positively with an action plan

Instructions:

1. **Choose a Roleplay Partner.** Enlist a spouse, friend, or family member to partner with. Roleplaying allows realistic rehearsal without real-world stakes.
2. **Decide on Roles and Scenarios.** One of you will play *"parent"* and the other *"teacher."* Then, discuss a scenario—*is academics, behavior, or social issues the main concern?* Set the context.
3. **Gather "Parent" Talking Points.** As the *"parent,"* reflect on two to three priority issues you want to discuss and evidence that demonstrates them. Make some notes to reference as needed.
4. **Set the Tone.** Have the *"parent"* initiate the roleplay by warmly introducing themselves and setting a collaborative tone upfront.
5. **Act Out the Conference.** Roleplay a realistic conference using the scenario you outlined. The *"teacher"* can offer perspectives and feedback based on the concern. Use your talking points, but speak conversationally.

6. **Practice Raising Issues Diplomatically.** Pay attention to tactfully expressing concerns while demonstrating goodwill, like *"I want to be upfront about some struggles we have noticed, and I know we both want what is best for my child."*
7. **Discuss Accommodations and Solutions.** Suggest accommodations like preferential seating or extended time on assignments. Respond positively as the *"teacher"* proposes ideas. End with an action plan.
8. **Wrap Up Professionally.** Conclude the roleplay by recapping the next steps and thanking the *"teacher"* for their partnership.
9. **Switch Roles.** Have your partner play *"parent"* for a different scenario. Continue to alternate for more practice.

Debrief

Discuss reflections and takeaways from the exercise after you and your partner had turns in each role. *What skills felt natural? What was challenging? How will this help in actual conferences?*

Regularly rehearsing with a trusted partner equips you to master vital conferencing skills, including constructive concern-raising, solution-focused dialogue, finding common ground, and ending on a productive note. With practice, you will gain confidence to initiate partnerships with teachers and optimally support your child.

Chapter 9
Self-Care for Parents

With the cycle of doctor visits, educational consultations, missed assignments, and emotional highs and lows, it is too common to focus solely on making it through each day. Yet amid this tumultuous routine, prioritizing one's well-being is far from a luxury; it is an essential part of effective parenting.

This chapter underscores the vital role self-care plays for parents, specifically in raising a child with ADHD. Remember, *pausing to invest in personal health and mental resilience is not a sign of selfishness—it is a prerequisite for being an emotionally available and effective parent.*

With proper self-care, raising a child with ADHD can become more manageable, rewarding, and, ultimately, more successful for the entire family.

Putting on Your Oxygen Mask First

The familiar airline safety spiel says, *"Put on your own oxygen mask before assisting others."* This analogy applies perfectly to parenting a child. As your child's parent, your health, well-being, and sanity must come first before you can be fully present and care for your child.

Perhaps it sounds easier said than done, especially for parents of kids with special needs. The demands on your time and attention never seem to end. But even small steps to regularly renew your spirit will make a big difference. You deserve to have outlets that bring you joy and serenity amidst the demands of parenting. *Every child needs their parents at their best.*

The Effects of Caregiver Burnout

Caring for a child with ADHD takes immense mental and emotional energy. The constant alertness to stay on top of symptoms and behaviors can slowly lead parents to burnout if they are not careful. Some common signs of caregiver burnout include:

- Feeling emotionally drained or overwhelmed by the responsibilities of caregiving.
- Mental and physical exhaustion that makes it difficult to complete daily tasks.
- Increased irritability that leads to frequent outbursts of anger or frustration.
- Diminished patience and empathy.
- Sadness, depression, or hopelessness.
- Increased social isolation and withdrawal from relationships.
- Anxiety, chronic worry, and racing thoughts.
- Changes in appetite or sleep habits.
- Feeling like nothing you do as a caregiver makes a real difference.
- Health concerns like frequent headaches, stomach problems, or weakened immune system.
- Resentment towards your child or role as a caregiver.
- Thoughts of wanting to abandon your caregiving responsibilities.

If untreated, burnout can seriously impact your mental and physical health. It also affects your ability to provide consistent, loving care for your child. Irritability and loss of empathy mean kids see less of your best qualities. *Burnout benefits no one.*

Why "Me Time" Matters

From the moment you open your eyes in the morning until you finally find a few moments of stillness at night, your world revolves around those you cherish the most: *your kids*. Often, in the whirlwind of parenthood, your needs become background noise, easy to dismiss amidst the daily demands.

But here is a gentle reminder from one parent to another: *You are not just a caregiver but a person with dreams, feelings, and needs.* Taking time for yourself is about recharging, finding your center, and reminding yourself of who you are beyond the parent role. Once you are recharged, you can listen attentively, love more deeply, and be more present.

Below are the benefits of taking a step back and practicing self-care.

Improved Mental Health

Chronic stress, burnout, and trying to do it all often breed anxiety and depression. By contrast, relaxing and recharging through activities like yoga, massages, quiet reading time, or bubble baths gives your mind a much-needed break. Self-care boosts feel-good endorphins, calms worry, and lifts mood. Your overall mental health and outlook improve exponentially.

Increased Patience and Energy

When stuck in crisis mode without breaks, your patience wears thin. Little frustrations can set you off because your energy is drained. Taking time for self-care helps prevent this. Simple renewals like walking, playing with a pet, or journaling help lengthen your fuse.

Strengthened Relationships

Neglecting your needs causes relationships to suffer. Spouses feel disconnected because all your time and energy goes to the kids. At the same time, friendships may fall by the wayside.

Being out a couple of times, girls' nights out, date nights, or trips with friends strengthens these critical bonds. It reminds partners and friends they still matter, which nurtures those relationships.

Improved Parenting

Studies consistently show that self-care makes parents feel more confident, focused, and purposeful. When your cup is full, you have a greater capacity to connect with your child, implement parenting strategies, and handle meltdowns patiently. It gives you the inner energy to listen, empathize, and respond thoughtfully rather than just reacting. *Fulfilling your own needs first allows you to meet their needs.*

Healthier Image for Kids

Seeing you take time for yourself models self-care skills for your children as they grow. They see first-hand how nurturing yourself recharges your batteries and leaves you more available to give to others. Setting these healthy boundaries also implicitly permits your child to do the same. Set as an example.

Greater Life Balance and Joy

Self-care allows you to cultivate all aspects of your life, not just parenthood. Make time for hobbies, creativity outlets, learning new skills, nurturing faith, advancing your career, and physical activity—all core parts of your being. This life balance boosts joy and satisfaction.

When fulfilled across different areas, you approach parenting with greater contentment and presence. Your joy becomes infectious.

Improved Physical Health

Many self-care activities like exercise, nutritious meals, massage, and quality sleep directly aid physical health. However, reducing parenting stress through self-care alleviates inflammation, headaches, stomach troubles, and blood pressure issues. Taking time to move your body, cook healthy foods, and unwind positively impacts your well-being from head to toe. Being in your best health allows you to keep up with your kids.

Better Self-Worth and Confidence

When you continuously put yourself last, it erodes your self-worth. Self-care sends the message that you matter. Setting these needed boundaries, making time for your passions, and nurturing your health builds confidence.

Realize your immeasurable worth beyond just being someone's parent. That self-assuredness makes you a stronger, happier guardian.

Self-Care Strategies for Parents

Without intervention, caregiver burnout only gets worse. It sabotages physical and mental health while eroding your ability to parent effectively. Studies show burned-out parents are more likely to develop clinical depression or anxiety. The risks extend to your child, too, with increased behavioral issues and poorer academic performance.

Carving out *"me time"* can feel impossible with the demands of parenting, especially for a child with additional needs. But even short rests help strengthen your will to handle challenges. Your health and well-being matter, so here are tips for practicing self-care.

Give Yourself Permission to Rest

Parents especially often feel guilty for taking time to rest and recover. But periods of complete rest, where you relinquish all responsibilities and to-do's, are essential.

Learn to Say "No"

A huge cause of burnout is saying yes to everyone and everything. Self-care requires getting comfortable saying no sometimes so you do not overextend yourself. Be choosy about which activities and commitments fit your schedule without pushing you into burnout territory. Give yourself permission to decline or remove optional extras that feel burdensome.

When your friend asks for a favor, but you have plans to read and take a bubble bath—decline politely. When your child asks you to volunteer for the PTA on top of everything else, it is okay to say no.

Accept that you cannot do it all, and be realistic about what you can handle. Do not feel guilty for needing rest. Lastly, protect your energy by setting boundaries around your capacity.

Reclaim Your Weekends

For working parents especially, weekends can become a crash course in catching up on chores, errands, and all the tasks you couldn't get to during the work week. While getting things done is essential, resist the urge to overschedule.

Protect a good chunk of time to relax and have fun alone or with family. Permit yourself to lounge in your pajamas all morning, take a day trip somewhere new, explore a favorite hobby, or binge-watch a show. Feeding your soul is as necessary as checking things off your to-do list.

Plan Regular Getaways

In addition to daily and weekend self-care, schedule regular vacations and getaways throughout the year. Having longer breaks to look forward to is huge for stress management and your overall mindset.

Get input from your whole family on trip ideas. Either go camping, hit amusement parks, rent a cozy cabin in the woods, or lounge at the beach—choose destinations that help everyone recharge.

If packing up for overnight trips feels too much, plan regular day trips to give you and your kids a change of scenery.

Outsource Help When Possible

Take advantage of any help you can get from others. Tap into family, friends, or your community resources for additional support. Do not be afraid to ask for help or accept help when offered. For instance:

- Have groceries delivered versus spending hours shopping and errand running.
- Hire a mother's helper or babysitter for a few hours of relief.
- Swap childcare with other parents for mom's day out.
- Seek academic tutors or therapists to support your child's needs.

- Hire a cleaning service instead of DIYing everything.
- Ask your spouse or older kids to cover certain household duties.
- Swap childcare with other parents.
- Pay for extracurricular transportation if driving is a burden.

Exercise and Move Your Body

Exercise has physical and mental health benefits. As little as 30 minutes of daily activity can improve your mood, outlook, stress levels, and sleep.

Any movement counts, such as taking an exercise class, swimming, biking, doing yoga, or playing active games as a family. Identify forms of exercise you enjoy and turn them into a daily habit.

Eat Nutritious Foods

A balanced, nutritious diet directly fuels your capacity to handle stress and function at your best. Meal prep ahead of time so you have healthy grabs like:

- Yogurt parfaits
- Veggies and hummus
- Fruit and nut trail mix
- Hard-boiled eggs
- Smoothies or protein shakes

Limit sugar, excessive carbs, and caffeine, which can heighten anxiety. Getting good nutrition will nourish you physically and mentally.

Prioritize Quality Sleep

Sleep is hugely restorative, yet it is usually the first thing parents sacrifice when life gets busy. Do all you can to get seven to nine hours of quality sleep per night. Maintain a soothing bedtime routine that primes your body to relax. Limit electronics and screen time before bed. Invest in comfortable bedding and blackout curtains. Getting your sleep back on track will make you more patient, focused, and purposeful in your daily life.

Seek Community Support

Connect with other parents who understand the rewards and challenges of raising an ADHD child. There is no need to walk this path alone. There is strength and comfort in the community. You can:

- Join an ADHD parent support group.
- Participate in online forums to exchange stories and advice.
- Open up to trusted friends and family members.
- Consider counseling to process difficult emotions.

Remember Your "Why"

When your energy is low, remember why you do this parenting thing in the first place. Your child is amazing and one-of-a-kind. Focus on the moments that fill your heart, like:

- Cuddling up, reading bedtime stories
- Celebrating developmental milestones
- Laughing together at silly jokes
- Seeing your child show empathy and kindness

Even on the hardest days, do not forget the profound gifts of parenting this beautiful child. Keeping your motivation front and center makes the self-care journey so worthwhile.

Managing Stress

While self-care establishes needed boundaries and nurtures your overall well-being, stress management is about building resilience daily and in the moment. It gives you tools to prevent constant stressors like tantrums, lack of focus, school struggles, and more from pushing you to the breaking point.

The aim is to buffer yourself from the avalanche of stressors through healthy habits and coping mechanisms. Whether it is deep breathing when frustration hits, limiting social media, or maintaining perspective—with the right stress-busting toolbox, you can master your mindset and avoid burnout.

Think of stress management as the yin to self-care's yang—complementary forces that allow you to withstand the marathon of raising your unique child. So, in addition to taking guilt-free time for yourself, build your capacity to roll with the punches that life throws at you. Here are strategies for empowered, resilient stress management as a parent of a child with ADHD:

Start a Daily Stress-Busting Routine

Carve out 20 to 30 minutes every day for activities shown to reverse stress. Try rotating through these go-to stress busters:

- **Exercise.** Boosts feel-good endorphins and improves sleep.
- **Meditation.** Lowers blood pressure and calms the mind.
- **Yoga.** Relieves tension through stretching and focused breathing.

- **Nature time.** Fresh air and sunshine are healing.
- **Listening to music.** Soothes anxiety and lifts mood instantly.
- **Taking a hot shower or bath.** The water eases muscle tension.
- **Reading fiction.** Gets your mind off real-life worries.
- **Journaling.** Helps process emotions and thoughts.

Choose a few favorites and do them regularly. Combine a few each day for maximum impact. This takes your attention away from stressors.

Limit News and Social Media

Today's nonstop news cycle and doomscrolling through social media exacerbate stress and anxiety. Set limits on your exposure for better peace of mind.

Designate news to certain times of day, like right when you wake up and in the evening. Avoid screens for an hour before bedtime. Temporarily mute friends sharing constant bad news. Follow more positive, uplifting accounts that make you smile.

Be choosy about your information diet to control its effects on your psyche. *The more you can minimize stressors, the better.*

Learn Quick Calming Techniques

When stress strikes at the moment, use these quick tricks to regain composure:

- Take five deep, slow breaths. Inhale for a 5 count, exhale for a 5 count.
- Count backward slowly from 100. Focus only on the numbers.

- Engage your senses. Look around and name five things you see.
- Allow yourself to feel it fully. Say, *"This too shall pass."*
- Splash cool water on your face or the back of your neck.
- Diffuse calming essential oils like lavender.
- Give yourself a hand or shoulder massage.
- Play a funny video for a few minutes of relief.

Reframe Your Perspective

How you perceive challenging circumstances is everything. When something stressful happens, try reframing it in a more positive light.

For example, a public tantrum could easily ruin your whole day. Or you could take comfort that this too shall pass; your child is learning, and tomorrow is a new day. Focus on the bigger picture rather than getting mired in the moment.

Look for nuggets of wisdom or humor whenever possible. Laugh at the absurdity life throws your way sometimes. Cultivating resilient thinking takes practice but prevents stress from getting catastrophic.

Set Healthy Boundaries

Burnout often stems from a lack of boundaries in your work or home life. To dial back stress:

- Learn to say no if your plate is full.
- Be firm about your needs and limitations.
- Ask directly for what you require.
- Communicate priorities and allow others to support them.
- Let go of people-pleasing tendencies.
- Outsource tasks that drain you.
- Discuss workload concerns and stressors with your manager.

- Set office hours and mute work email or chat off-hours.

Make Time for Fun and Connection

Make time for activities that spark joy and nurture your relationships. Share laughs with your friends. Get lost in a favorite hobby like gardening or painting. Play board games as a family or binge-watch a hilarious show. Download a goofy TikTok dance and master it.

Feed your spirit with play, creativity, and quality time with your loved ones. Do not let stress make life all about grinding.

Go Easy on Yourself

Stress and burnout often stem from unrealistic expectations of yourself as parents. Counteract this with plenty of self-compassion. When you are obsessing over a mistake or imperfection, ask yourself: *would I talk to my best friend this way?* **Treat yourself kindly.**

Remind yourself every parent has slip-ups and struggles sometimes. You are doing the best you can, and that is enough. Let go of perfectionism and realize progress over perfection is what matters most on this parenting journey.

Share Your Feelings with Others

Do not experience parenting alone. Connecting with family, friends, and other parents for moral support can ease feelings of stress and isolation.

Share your biggest worries and frustrations with your spouse or close friends. Join an ADHD parent support group. Set up regular play dates or mom's nights out. Ask grandparents if they can help with childcare.

Knowing there are others who understand what you are going through is hugely comforting. Never underestimate the value of community.

Make Stress Management a Priority

Do not wait for stress to become unmanageable. Nip it in the bud by trying one new coping strategy today, then build consistency.

Between daily relief habits, shifting perspective, outlets for fun, and more— you have so many tools! Be compassionate with yourself, and realize progress over perfection is the goal. Combating chronic stress takes commitment, but every step counts.

Exercise: The Stress Test

Stress can easily sneak up. That is why checking in with yourself and honestly assessing your current stress levels is necessary.

Below is a simple stress test. Rate how often you have experienced common stress symptoms. Your total score will indicate whether your stress levels are healthy or reaching more dangerous levels requiring attention.

Instructions:

Think about the past week and rate each of the following symptoms on a scale of 0 to 5:

- 0 = Never/Rarely
- 1 = Occasionally
- 2 = Sometimes
- 3 = Often
- 4 = Very Often
- 5 = Constantly

Questionnaire:

- ___ Feeling irritable or easily annoyed
- ___ Feeling anxious/nervous
- ___ Lacking motivation
- ___ Fatigue/low energy
- ___ Poor sleep quality
- ___ Increased alcohol/drug use
- ___ Withdrawing from responsibilities
- ___ Feeling sad or hopeless
- ___ Muscle tension or headaches
- ___ Stomach troubles
- ___ Changes in appetite
- ___ Increased conflict with others
- ___ Difficulty concentrating
- ___ Racing thoughts
- ___ Crying spells
- ___ Sweating or tremors
- ___ Teeth grinding
- ___ Dizziness/nausea

Interpretation:

If your total score is:

- 0 to 20: Low stress
- 21 to 40: Moderate stress
- 41 to 70: High stress
- Over 70: Extremely high stress

When you score ***over 70***, this indicates extremely high stress levels requiring prompt care. Make self-care an immediate priority and seek professional help.

For scores ranging from ***41 to 70***, your stress is elevated, and self-care strategies could help lower your stress.

Then, if scored ***under 40***, stress is normal, but be proactive with self-care.

Retake this assessment weekly or monthly to monitor your stress levels over time. Tracking your stress empowers you to intervene early when life gets too overwhelming.

Conclusion

Throughout this book, numerous aspects of understanding and navigating ADHD in children have been addressed. The aim has been to offer practical strategies and insights to smooth the parenting journey. Having gone through various topics—*from defining ADHD to discussing its prevalence and offering management techniques*—this book is a comprehensive toolkit for parents.

The journey started with understanding what ADHD is and its widespread impact, laying the groundwork for subsequent chapters. Following that, the book delved into behavioral management techniques based on understanding children's specific needs. Topics such as resilience, structuring an ADHD-friendly environment, and the importance of routines were explored. The value of positive reinforcement, rewards, effective communication, and empathy was also underscored. Special attention was given to the role of schools and how collaboration can enhance a child's development. Additionally, the importance of parental self-care was emphasized as being crucial for being an effective caregiver.

This comprehensive approach intends to empower parents to feel confident in managing the challenges and appreciating the joys of raising a child with ADHD. While the condition presents obstacles, it also brings immense potential for creativity, energy, and intuition. With the right support and understanding, these unique qualities can truly shine.

As this book ends, remember that learning is a continuous process, and each child and situation is unique. Challenges should be viewed as opportunities to expand the toolkit of strategies. Over time, small steps of progress can lead to significant growth.

Progress may feel slow, but it is there. Lean on a community of support—parents, teachers, coaches, and other caregivers—because no one needs to walk this path alone. Support groups and shared experiences can offer invaluable help.

Although this book has offered a starting point, the journey of learning and adapting is never-ending. Continue to grow alongside your child, applying what has been useful and remaining open to new approaches. The importance of meeting each moment without judgment and with an open heart cannot be overstated.

Remember progress over perfection. There will be highs and lows, good days and bad. What matters is your commitment to show up with an open heart. Meet each moment as it comes without judgment. Let go of ideals and expectations. Your child is exactly who they need to be. Focus on nurturing their gifts and providing support where needed. The rest will fall into place.

Finally, believe in your child's potential. Hold the vision that they can achieve their biggest dreams. See them for all that they are beyond any label. Help them see their limitless possibilities too. Instill confidence by focusing on their strengths. Then equip them with tools to navigate difficulties when they inevitably arise. With the right support system in place, they can accomplish anything. The path may look different than expected but will be just as beautiful. Trust the journey.

Resources

Capodieci, A., & Re, A. M. (2020). Understanding ADHD: A Guide to Symptoms, Management and Treatment. Routledge.

Daniels, A. C. (2000). Bringing Out the Best in People. McGraw Hill Professional.

Grossberg, B., PsyD. (2015). Focused: ADHD & ADD Parenting Strategies for Children with Attention Deficit Disorder. Callisto Media.

Hamlet, H. S. (2016). School Counseling Practicum and Internship: 30 Essential Lessons. SAGE Publications.

Institute of Medicine. (2015). Transforming the Workforce for Children Birth Through Age 8: A Unifying Foundation. National Academies Press.

Klein, T. P. (2014). How Toddlers Thrive: What Parents Can Do Today for Children Ages 2-5 to Plant the Seeds of Lifelong Success. Simon and Schuster.

Mamta, & Bhatnagar, N. (2011). Effective Communication and Soft Skills. Pearson Education India.

Merrett, F., & Wheldall, K. (2017). Positive Teaching: The Behavioural Approach. Routledge.

My ADHD Pal. (2023). Conquering ADHD: Daily Practices for Focus, Clarity, and Success in Adult Life. Lulu.com.

O'Brien, K., & Chronis-Tuscano, A. (2020). Supporting Caregivers of Children with ADHD: An Integrated Parenting Program, Therapist Guide. Oxford University Press.

Park, V., & Datnow, A. (2018). Professional Collaboration with Purpose: Teacher Learning Towards Equitable and Excellent Schools. Routledge.

Pastor, P. N. (2015). Association Between Diagnosed ADHD and Selected Characteristics Among Children Aged 4-17 Years, United States, 2011-2013. U.S. Department of Health and Human Services, Centers for Disease Control and Prevention, National Center for Health Statistics.

Rakel, D. (2012). Integrative Medicine. Elsevier Health Sciences.

Rothstein, D., & Santana, L. (2016). Partnering with Parents to Ask the Right Questions: A Powerful Strategy for Strengthening School-Family Partnerships. ASCD.

Safo, M. (Mrs.). (2006). The Mirror: Issue 2,704 October 14, 2006. Graphic Communications Group.

Schmitz, T. J., & O'Sullivan, S. B. (2019). Physical Rehabilitation. F.A. Davis.

Shea, V., & Mesibov, G. B. (2010). The TEACCH Approach to Autism Spectrum Disorders. Springer Science & Business Media.

Visconti, P. J., & Statkiewicz Sherer, M. A. (2021). Radiation Protection in Medical Radiography - E-Book. Elsevier Health Sciences.

Weiss, S. K., & Heininger, J. E. (2001). From Chaos to Calm: Effective Parenting for Challenging Children with ADHD and Other Behavioral Problems. Penguin.

Brown, T. E. (2013). A New Understanding of ADHD in Children and Adults: Executive Function Impairments. Routledge.

Techniques Recap

The following techniques are found in *"How to Parent Children with ADHD:"*

#	Technique/Tip Name	Explanation
1	Rewards for Desired Behaviors	Provide tokens or points as rewards for demonstrating desired behaviors.
2	Practicing Desired Responses	Practice desired responses in simulated real-life situations.
3	Behavior Tracking	Have the child track their behaviors and habits to increase self-awareness.
4	Learning Organizational Systems	Teach the child systems like checklists and planners to stay on task.
5	Regular Aerobic Exercise	Engage in regular aerobic exercise to burn excess energy and improve focus and cognitive performance.
6	Nutritious Diet	Prepare a nutritious, protein-rich diet for optimal brain function.
7	Consistent Schedules	Maintain consistent schedules for meals, homework, and bedtime.
8	Minimizing Distractions	Structure home and workspace to minimize distractions.
9	Knowledge Empowerment	Gain knowledge about ADHD to understand and respond compassionately to behaviors.
10	Understanding ADHD	Learn about the nature of ADHD for insight into your child's challenges.

How to Parent Children with ADHD

#	Technique/Tip Name	Explanation
11	Simplifying Directions	Give only one direction at a time.
12	Using Timers	Set timers for work periods, like 30 minutes, to improve focus.
13	Writing Down Assignments	Have the child write down assignment instructions and due dates.
14	Tackling Harder Work Early	Do challenging tasks like math and reading when the child's focus is best.
15	Engaging with Questions	Keep the child engaged by asking frequent questions.
16	Praising Good Behavior	Praise good behavior and effort.
17	Energy Release Breaks	Allow quick breaks every 20 to 30 minutes during long tasks for energy release.
18	Using Fidget Toys	Let the child keep small fidget toys at their desk for restless hands.
19	Teaching Coping Techniques	Teach techniques like deep breathing or visualization for stress management.
20	Demonstrating Decision-Making	Model thoughtful decision-making.
21	Patient Reactions	React patiently to behaviors, using them as teaching moments.
22	Modeling Patience	Use patience as a tool to model self-control.
23	Encouraging Optimism	Reframe challenges and focus on progress for optimism.
24	Teaching Adaptability	Highlight the ever-changing nature of life and encourage adaptable responses.
25	Instilling Self-Belief	Emphasize past successes and frame capabilities as learnable skills.

#	Technique/Tip Name	Explanation
26	Encouraging Seeking Help	Normalize needing support and build a support group.
27	Instilling Hope	Share stories of individuals who have overcome challenges, especially those with ADHD.
28	Hope Journal	Initiate a 'Hope Journal' for writing down hopes, dreams, and worries.
29	Observing and Verbalizing Positives	Regularly identify and verbalize your child's positive qualities.
30	Expressing Unconditional Love	Show warmth and love through words, hugs, and quality time.
31	Activity Coordination	Coordinate activities around the child's interests.
32	Setting Attainable Goals	Set challenging yet attainable goals to build resilience.
33	Creating Specific Activity Areas	Designate specific areas for different activities.
34	Adapting Strategies	Be ready to adapt strategies as the child grows.
35	Understanding Sensory Experiences	Create an environment where the child feels understood in their sensory experience.
36	Using Rules as Guides	Frame rules and expectations as guides for behavior.
37	Consistency in Rules	Follow through consistently with established rules.
38	Using Visual Aids	Employ visual aids to help follow daily routines.
39	Resetting Routines	Reset and recommit to routines without shaming for past lapses.

#	Technique/Tip Name	Explanation
40	Substitute Routines	Have alternative routines for unexpected days like sick or snow days.
41	Balancing Reinforcement and Consequences	Use positive reinforcement but also let the child face natural consequences.
42	Balancing Reward Types	Combine tangible rewards with other types for holistic motivation.
43	Open Communication	Maintain open communication as a trust pillar in the relationship.
44	Respecting Different Experiences	Respect and reframe behaviors often seen as defiance.
45	Observing Situational Cues	Look for situational cues when the child has difficulty vocalizing.
46	Embracing Silence	Learn to embrace silent moments in communication.
47	Collaborating with Teachers	Build partnerships with teachers for aligned support and insight.
48	Prioritizing Parental Health	Focus on your own health and well-being to be fully present for your child.

Exclusive Bonuses

Dear Parents,

As you navigate the rewarding yet challenging path of parenting a child with ADHD, I am delighted to present you with five special bonuses. These resources are tailored to support and enrich your journey, offering practical insights and tools to help you and your child thrive.

- **Bonus 1 - Journey of Understanding: A Parent's Diary on Raising Children with ADHD**
  This diary serves as a compassionate companion, offering reflections and insights from fellow parents. It's a space for you to connect with shared experiences, gather wisdom, and find solace in the community of parents on similar paths.

- **Bonus 2 - Growing Together: A Progress Tracker for Parenting Children with ADHD**
  This tracker is designed to help you monitor and celebrate your child's milestones and progress. It includes customizable charts and tools to track improvements, setbacks, and strategies that work, fostering a sense of achievement and direction.

- **Bonus 3 - Deciphering ADHD: A Parent's Flowchart Guide to Identifying ADHD in Children**
  This guide provides a visual, step-by-step flowchart to help you understand and identify signs of ADHD in children. It simplifies the process of recognition, making it easier to seek timely support and intervention.

- **Bonus 4 - Tailored Connections: A Parenting Style Quiz for Parents of Children with ADHD**
  Discover your unique parenting style with this insightful quiz. It helps you recognize your strengths and areas for growth, enabling you to adapt your approach to meet your child's specific needs effectively.

- **Bonus 5 - Delightful Bites: ADHD-Friendly Treat Recipes for Kids**
  Enjoy this collection of healthy, delicious, and easy-to-make treat recipes designed for children with ADHD. These recipes focus on nutritious ingredients that can support focus and overall well-being.

How to Access Your Bonuses:

Scan the QR Code Below: Use your smartphone to scan the QR code, and you'll be taken directly to the bonus content.

Visit the Link: You can also access these valuable resources by visiting our dedicated website link: https://bit.ly/Laine-ADHD (Attention: The link is case-sensitive. Enter the link exactly as it is, with the correct uppercase and lowercase letters. Otherwise, the link will not work properly)

These bonuses are crafted to provide you with additional support, understanding, and resources as you embark on this parenting journey. Embrace each step with confidence, knowing you're not alone.

Warmest regards,

Krissa Laine

Made in United States
Orlando, FL
02 March 2025